Puppet Scripts

for Preschool Worship

Ages 3-6

Violet M. Toler

Standard
PUBLISHING
Bringing The Word to Life™

Cincinnati, Ohio

Puppet Scripts for Preschool Worship

Written by Violet M. Toler
Edited by Christina Wallace
Cover design by Becky Hawley
Interior design by Andrew Quach
Illustrations of Scout and Scamper by Kathryn Marlin

Standard Publishing, Cincinnati, Ohio.
A division of Standex International Corporation.
© 2005 by Standard Publishing
All rights reserved.
Printed in the United States of America

12 11 10 09 08 07 06 05   5 4 3 2 1

ISBN 0-7847-1782-6

Table of Contents

• Special Features for Teachers

• Old Testament Scripts

• New Testament

• Holidays & Special Seasons

Introduction
to Preschool/Pre-K & K Children

In order to effectively teach preschool/pre-K & K children, it is important to understand how they are developing physically, intellectually, emotionally, socially, and spiritually. When teachers reach out to children at their levels, children are more engaged and are better able to grasp important Bible truths. *Puppet Scripts for Preschool Worship* focuses on each of these five areas of development.

Physically

Preschool children

* can't sit still
* need a lot of physical play and space
* have one-track minds but can be distracted

Pre-K & K children

* are wiggly but are learning to sit still
* are rapidly developing coordination
* are physically growing fast

In *Puppet Scripts for Preschool Worship,* Scout and Scamper interact with children by inviting them to move, sing, and answer questions. The scripts incorporate objects that Scout and Scamper discuss or manipulate, helping to keep kids engaged.

Intellectually

Preschool children

* have unlimited questions, especially "Why?"
* learn by actual experiences
* have short attention spans and need rotated activities

Pre-K & K children

* think concretely and playact experiences
* like to explore and are curious
* like big words, and their vocabulary is growing fast

In *Puppet Scripts for Preschool Worship,* the scripts are brief and focused for short attention spans. The puppets help children learn the answers to important questions like *Why should I obey? How can I show kindness? and What does it mean to follow Jesus?* Scripts include questions for guided discussions to help children process what they learn and apply it to their lives.

Emotionally

Preschool children

* are generally self-centered but naturally loving
* are determined and shouldn't be discouraged
* have rapidly changing emotions

Pre-K & K children

- love to please, especially adults
- love repetition and routine, which give them security
- have great imaginations and are creative

In *Puppet Scripts for Preschool Worship,* children learn along with the puppets how to care for others and why kindness pleases God. Children become familiar with Scout and Scamper and are more comfortable coming to worship, excited to learn new Bible truths. Children use their imaginations as they step into Scout and Scamper's world for a short time during each class.

Socially

Preschool children

- imitate others, so good examples are important
- are uninhibited and need protection
- play independently, side by side

Pre-K & K children

- are becoming very social and are making friends at church
- relate to the world from their experiences
- can be boisterous and noisy but can learn limits

In *Puppet Scripts for Preschool Worship,* Scout and Scamper provide an example for children as the puppets learn from their playful predicaments. Children see Scout and Scamper learning and understand that although the puppets are growing, like themselves, they still need others to care for them. Children learn self-control as they watch the puppets learn from various situations.

Spiritually

Preschool children

- are learning what God did and who Jesus is
- know the Bible is a special book about God and Jesus
- understand that prayer is talking to God, and God listens to their prayers

Pre-K & K children

- are learning more details about what God did and who Jesus is
- know the Bible is a special, true book about God and Jesus
- understand that God is good, loves them all the time, is powerful

In *Puppet Scripts for Preschool Worship,* children learn about God and how much He loves them. Children learn important Bible truths along with Scout and Scamper. Scout and Scamper learn and help children understand what it means to serve God.

Using Puppets in the Classroom

Why use puppets in your classroom? Because using puppets in your classroom each week adds interest, energy, and a new friend for the children.

Hand puppets can be used in a preschool classroom to

- greet the children as they arrive
- help gather the children for the Bible story time
- sing with the children
- bring in props for a Bible story
- act out the application story

A warm, friendly puppet can help you in other ways too. Use a puppet when

- making announcements or handing out award stickers
- acknowledging children's answers to questions
- giving encouragement to children
- leading in cleanup or saying good-bye

If a child feels uncomfortable talking to or asking questions of the teacher, she may be willing to talk to a puppet.

Before you use a puppet in the classroom for the first time, practice with the puppet in front of a mirror. See if you can get the puppet to

- hug/kiss
- jump/run
- wave
- nod
- cry/wipe tears
- act surprised
- hide/cover eyes
- peer back and forth

Also practice other actions appropriate to the character of the puppet.

A puppet doesn't need to speak aloud. Nor does it need to appear from behind a puppet stage. Simply hold the puppet and let it whisper in your ear. Then tell the children what the puppet has told or asked you. A puppet can also be used to act out situations. It can

- whisper to you and acknowledge positive actions children do
- cower when the classroom becomes too noisy
- act out getting along with others
- act out emotions felt during stressful times

Children love puppets and respond to them in delightful ways. Have fun with puppets and let them help you lead playful children in learning about their great and loving God.

Meet
Scout and Scamper

Meet Scout and Scamper, the preschool/pre-K & K puppet friends! Scout and Scamper want to be a part of each week's lesson activities. Get to know each puppet and feel free to develop their personalities further in class!

Here Comes Scamper!

There are lots of ways in which this cuddly little squirrel is just like your young children. Scamper is

- playful and fun
- energetic and active (a climber and a jumper)
- curious and likes to explore (but sometimes gets into trouble doing so)
- easily excitable

Scamper lives in a tree in a backyard (anywhere!). He can jump fences and finds adventure throughout the neighborhood and in the woods nearby. He has a large family including his mother and several cousins. He loves nature, although he is afraid of water (lakes, ponds, and so forth). He likes to collect little things such as dandelions, leaves, and acorns. He learns quickly and likes to share what he knows with his best friend Scout.

Scout Is on the Prowl!

This energetic sheepdog is just like your classroom's children in lots of ways. Scout

- desires to please others
- offers love and affection
- can be stubborn at times
- is spirited
- can learn to obey

Scout lives in a doghouse in his people family's backyard, and he's always hunting for new adventures in the neighborhood. Scout is more knowledgeable about people than Scamper because Scout lives with people. Scout is always willing to share his favorite food, Puppy Crunch, with Scamper (who happens to think dog food is detestable). Scout loves playing with his best friend Scamper but at times can get too rough in his playfulness for the likes of the more laid-back squirrel.

God created curious squirrels, like Scamper, and playful sheepdogs, like Scout. Have fun with Scout and Scamper as they help you lead playful children in learning about their great and loving God.

How to Build Your Own Puppet Stage

Every puppet needs a good stage to set the tone and to help make the puppet seem believable, more realistic. The size of your stage will depend on the size of your room, how much time and energy you want to invest in preparing the stage, and perhaps the size of your budget. Below are options for building various puppet stages from quick and easy to larger, more involved sets. Choose the option that works best with your environment. Remember, with any set you can incorporate artificial trees to enhance the environment and make it more lifelike.

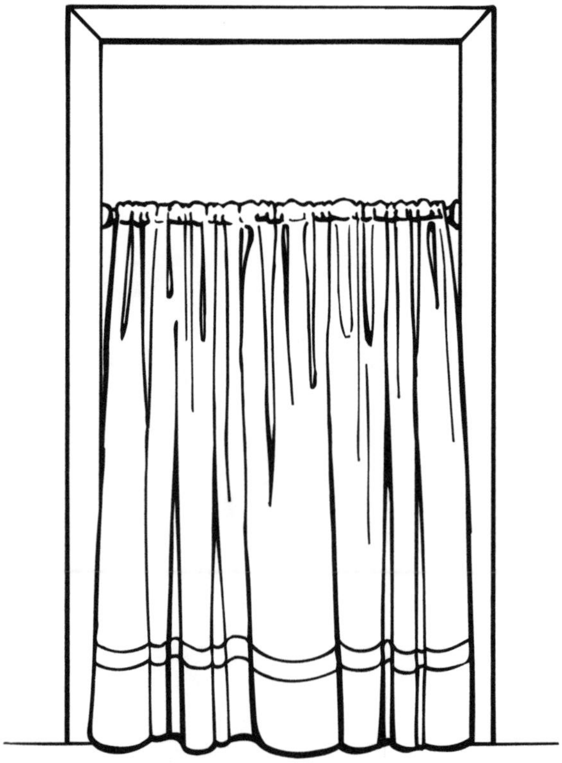

Stage #1

Supplies

- a doorway
- a tension rod that can fit inside the width of the doorway
- a curtain long enough to cover the bottom ¾ of the doorway (preferably dark)

Directions

For a quick and easy stage, hang a homemade curtain on a tension rod across a doorway (covering the bottom ¾ of the doorway). Scout and Scamper can appear above the curtain while the puppeteers are hidden behind the curtain.

Stage #2

Supplies

- 3—10' length 1½" PVC pipes cut to dimensions shown in the diagram
- 2—1½" 45° street elbow fittings
- 2—1½" 90° vent elbow fittings
- 2—1½" DWV Tee fittings
- 4—6" x 6" wooden bases with a hole drilled in the center of each to fit PVC pipes

- 4 yds.—heavy material cut into four 36" widths (curtain)
- needle, thread to match
- hot glue gun and sticks

Directions

Hem each section of material. Fold over the top of each curtain, and sew an 8" seam in which to insert the horizontal pipes. Assemble PVC pipes according to illustration. (It may take two people.) Hot glue sections together. Set legs into wooden bases for stability.

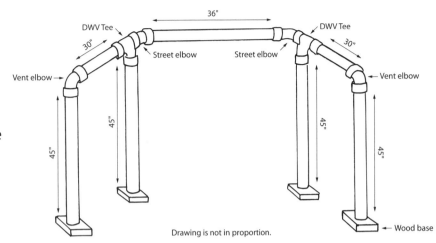

Stage #3

Supplies

- stage #2 fully assembled (see above)
- p. 131 copied onto a transparency
- overhead projector
- roll paper
- pencil
- paint (various colors, as desired for puppet background)
- paintbrushes (assorted sizes)

Directions

Attach roll paper to a wall. Project the transparency onto the paper using an overhead projector. Using the pencil, trace the projected image onto the paper. Paint using appropriate colors. Attach the mural to a wall behind and above the stage (stage #2). Puppets can appear above the curtain and in front of the mural so that it looks like they're in a backyard. Puppeteers can remain hidden behind the curtain.

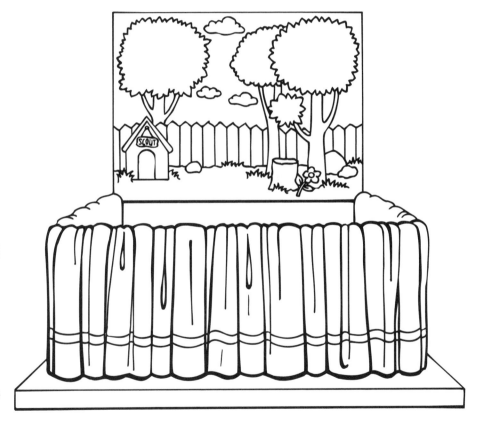

Stage #4

Supplies

- doghouse and tree from p. 132 copied onto separate transparencies
- overhead projector
- roll paper
- pencil or black marker
- paint (various colors, as desired for doghouse and tree)
- paintbrushes (assorted sizes)
- 10' lengths 1½" PVC pipes (as many as needed and cut to desired lengths to frame the tree and doghouse per the size you desire)
- 8—12" lengths 1½" PVC pipes
- 4—1½" 90° vent elbow fittings
- 4—DWV Tee fittings

Directions (follow the same directions for making the tree and/or the doghouse)

Attach roll paper to a wall (as much as needed for the size tree and doghouse you wish to make.) Using an overhead projector, project the transparencies of the tree and doghouse onto the paper. Trace the projected images onto the paper and paint using appropriate colors. Cut around the tree and doghouse in the shape of rectangles, leaving extra roll paper around the sides and tops to wrap around the frames.

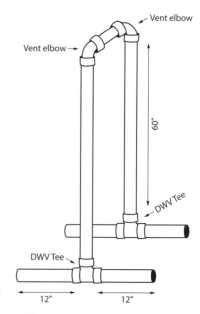

Drawing is not in proportion.

For each rectangle, create a frame using PVC pipe. Cut two long pieces (equal to the height of the tree or doghouse you've made) and one short piece (the width of the tree or doghouse you've made). Assemble the two sides and the top of the rectangle frame using the PVC pipes and two vent elbows. At the bottom of each side of the frame, attach a DWV Tee fitting. Insert 12" sections of PVC pipe (one into each side of the DWV Tee fittings) to make feet on each side of the frame. The feet will extend front to back of the frame.

Mount the tree and doghouse to the frames by wrapping the edges of the roll paper around the PVC pipes and securing them with tape so that the pipes are behind the image. Cut a hole in the treetop so that Scamper can appear in the tree. Cut a hole in the doghouse doorway so that Scout can appear from inside the doghouse. The puppeteers can hide behind each frame.

God Made the Sky and the Earth

Based on: Genesis 1—God Made the Sky and Earth
Props: none

Scamper: *(excited)* Hi, Scout! Did you see me jump from one tree to another?

Scout: I sure did! *(points and looks up)* You were high in the sky!

Scamper: It was fun!

Scout: It looked exciting.

Scamper: It felt like I was flying! *(spreads front paws and sways as though flying)* Wheee!

Scout: *(sadly)* Birds fly. Squirrels don't, and neither do dogs.

Scamper: I know, but when I leap through the air, it's almost like flying.

Scout: *(hangs head)* I can't climb trees or jump high in the sky.

Scamper: That's because you are not a squirrel.

Scout: I want to have fun too.

Scamper: Don't worry, Scout. We'll think of something fun you can do.

Scout: *(hesitantly)* I like to dig holes in the earth. Sometimes I hide a bone by burying it in the ground.

Scamper: I hide nuts in the ground. *(scratches head, thinking)* What else can you do?

Scout: I like to run.

Scamper: You run faster than the other puppies.

Scout: *(cheerfully)* I do, don't I? I like to dash across the yard!

Scamper: See? We both have fun! You play on the ground, and I play up high!

Scout: *(hopefully)* I wish we could play together.

Scamper: Would you like to race?

Scout: We can't, because I can only run on the ground.

Scamper: That's OK. I'll race in the treetops, and you'll race on the ground!

Scout: I'm glad that God made the sky and the earth.

Scamper: We will have fun playing in His world.

Scout: First one to the apple tree wins!

Discussion Questions

1. What can Scamper do that Scout cannot do?
2. How did Scamper and Scout play together?
3. What lights did God put in the nighttime sky?
4. What does God think about His world?
5. What can you put under the ground so that a plant will grow?
6. How can we show our thankfulness to God?

God Made Fish and Birds

Based on: Genesis 1—God Made Fish and Birds
Props: none

SCOUT: *(shakes himself)*

SCAMPER: Hey, what do you think you're doing? You're getting me all wet!

SCOUT: *(looks at Scamper)* Oops! Sorry, Scamper. I was shaking water off my fur.

SCAMPER: *(wipes face with paws)* That's OK. How did you get so wet?

SCOUT: I've been splashing in the pond!

SCAMPER: Oh. *(pauses)* Why?

SCOUT: It's fun! You should try it!

SCAMPER: No, thank you. I'd rather have fun in a tree.

SCOUT: What can you do in a tree that is fun?

SCAMPER: I can run and jump! I can see the birds.

SCOUT: It may be fun for you, but I can't climb trees.

SCAMPER: What is so fun at the pond?

SCOUT: I can splash in the water. I saw some little fish swimming.

SCAMPER: *(interested)* You did?

SCOUT: *(sadly)* I tried to play with them, but they all swam away.

SCAMPER: I guess fish don't like to play with dogs.

SCOUT: Nope! They swam away fast!

SCAMPER: If I try to play with the birds, they quickly fly away too.

SCOUT: I wonder why fish and birds go away from us?

SCAMPER: They don't know we won't harm them.

SCOUT: I called to them, "Come back, little fishes!" but they didn't.

SCAMPER: *(giggles)* Funny Scout! Fish can't understand dog language!

SCOUT: Oh . . . No, I guess they can't.

SCAMPER: We can still enjoy having them nearby.

SCOUT: I like to look at fish. They are good swimmers.

SCAMPER: Birds are pretty too. I like to hear them sing.

SCOUT: Me too, Scamper.

SCAMPER: God made fish and birds.

SCOUT: God did a good job, didn't He?

SCAMPER: He sure did, Scout!

Discussion Questions

1. What would not play with Scout?
2. What would not play with Scamper?
3. Who thought of making birds and fish?
4. How did God feel about what He had made?
5. How can you help take care of birds? fish?
6. How can we thank God for birds and fish?

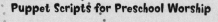

God Made All the Animals

Based on: Genesis 1—God Made Animals

Props: none

SCAMPER: Hi, Scout!

SCOUT: Hi, Scamper. I'm glad you are here. I want to ask you a question.

SCAMPER: OK, what is it?

SCOUT: How many kinds of animals are there?

SCAMPER: I don't know, but I think we can figure it out.

SCOUT: How can we know?

SCAMPER: We will count the animals.

SCOUT: That sounds like fun! I'm a dog. *(holds paw up)* Dogs are number one!

SCAMPER: Squirrels! That makes two!

SCOUT: Cats! Now we have three!

SCAMPER: Bears, big *(speaks in a gruff voice)* growly bears! Let's see, *(pauses)* I think that's four.

SCOUT: Long-necked giraffes!

SCAMPER: Don't forget monkeys! Now how many do we have?

SCOUT: Um, let's see. I said giraffes, then you said monkeys. How many did we have before that?

SCAMPER: Well . . . um, *(holds head and thinks)* we had four. Four plus two is . . . um . . .

SCOUT: Six! There are six kinds of animals! I remember another—wolves!

SCAMPER: But we forgot horses! That makes, *(pauses)* I forgot what number comes next.

SCOUT: Let me think. *(pauses)* Oh, I can't count right now. But I thought of more animals. There are sheep and goats!

SCAMPER: *(excited)* How about striped zebras and tigers?

SCOUT: There are mice too and cuddly pandas.

SCAMPER: *(slumps)* I'm getting tired, Scout. We've thought of a kazillion animals. Can we quit now?

SCOUT: I can think of others that we left out.

SCAMPER: We are never going to be able to count them all, but God knows the answer to your question.

SCOUT: God made all the animals!

SCAMPER: He knows them, every one.

Discussion Questions

1. What were Scout and Scamper counting?

2. Why couldn't Scout and Scamper count all the animals?

3. Who knows how many kinds of animals were created?

4. On which day did God create animals?

5. What is a wild animal that God made?

6. Which animal do you like best?

God Made the World

Based on: Genesis 1—God Made a World for People
Props: Place a few acorns nearby to show the children what small seeds acorns are compared to the large trees that grow from them.

Scamper:	Scout, you should see what happened to my acorn!
Scout:	What acorn?
Scamper:	The one I hid in the ground.
Scout:	*(impatient)* Scamper, you hide so many nuts, I can't know of each one.
Scamper:	This one is different.
Scout:	How is one nut different than the others?
Scamper:	Last fall I hid it at the edge of the yard and forgot about it.
Scout:	That was a year ago.
Scamper:	I know. I didn't uncover it in the winter.
Scout:	You uncovered a lot of them.
Scamper:	I did, and I ate them all.
Scout:	You forgot about this one?
Scamper:	Yep. I just remembered today and went to look for it.
Scout:	Was it still there?
Scamper:	It sure was, and it surprised me.
Scout:	How can a nut surprise a squirrel?

Scamper:	I'll tell you how! It grew into a baby tree!
Scout:	A baby tree? *(scratches head)* That is a mystery.
Scamper:	Scout, don't you know where trees come from?
Scout:	*(defensive)* They grow out of the ground.
Scamper:	That's right, but there is more to know.
Scout:	What else is there?
Scamper:	Acorns are seeds. They sprout into trees.
Scout:	*(skeptical)* Come on, Scamper. Trees are huge. You think they grow from a tiny nut?
Scamper:	I know they do. When the tree gets big, it makes lots more acorns.
Scout:	Wow! That is neat!
Scamper:	My big tree grows enough nuts for my family to eat. There are some left over to make new trees too.
Scout:	Did God plan that?
Scamper:	He did. God made the world.
Scout:	He thought of everything. *(giggles)* I wonder if He did that just for you squirrels?
Scamper:	I like to think so.
Scout:	Let's go see your baby tree.

Discussion Questions

1. What did Scamper bury?
2. What happened to Scamper's acorn?
3. Can you name a plant that God made?
4. What do you like most about the world that God made?
5. Who do you know who has a garden?
6. What good things grow in gardens?

God Made People

Based on: Genesis 1, 2—God Made People
Props: Place a small ear of corn next to Scamper.

SCAMPER: *(excited)* Hey, Scout! I found this corn hanging in my tree!

SCOUT: You can't fool me, Scamper! Corn doesn't grow on trees!

SCAMPER: I know, but it truly was there!

SCOUT: How did it happen?

SCAMPER: I don't know.

SCOUT: *(confidently)* I'll figure out who put it there.

SCAMPER: *(skeptical)* You can't know.

SCOUT: *(leans toward Scamper)* Come on, Scamper, answer one question. Where were you when the corn appeared?

SCAMPER: I was hiding in my nest inside the hollow tree. When I came out, there it was.

SCOUT: It wasn't there before?

SCAMPER: No, it wasn't. I was playing on that limb, then I ran to hide.

SCOUT: Were you playing hide-and-seek?

SCAMPER: No, I was afraid.

SCOUT: Why were you afraid?

SCAMPER: A *(emphasize)* big person came near.

SCOUT: *(laughs)* Even a child is big next to you, Scamper.

SCAMPER: *(feelings hurt)* Don't laugh at me, Scout! *(emphasize)* Everyone knows that *(emphasize)* all squirrels are afraid of people!

SCOUT: Sorry, Scamper. *(pauses)* My people are nice.

SCAMPER: Your people! You have people?

SCOUT: Yes, I have a man, a woman, and a little girl.

SCAMPER: Aren't you afraid of them?

SCOUT: Why should I be? They give me Puppy Crunch to eat. They brush my fur. *(wiggles)* Oh, it feels so good!

SCAMPER: *(surprised)* Really? They must like you a lot!

SCOUT: They do. They pat and play with me.

SCAMPER: *(wonderingly)* Maybe people aren't so bad, after all.

SCOUT: I think I know who gave you the corn.

SCAMPER: You do? Who?

SCOUT: A person.

SCAMPER: *(surprised)* No way!

SCOUT: Yes! People are good. God made people.

SCAMPER: I'm glad the person gave me corn to eat.

Discussion Questions

1. Why was Scamper afraid?
2. What food did the person give to Scamper?
3. Who made the first man and woman?
4. What food did God give to the man and woman?
5. Who made all of us?
6. What food do you like to eat?

God Made Our Bodies

Based on: Genesis 1, 2—God Made Adam and Eve
Props: Have a small apple sitting nearby. You may want to practice having Scamper hold the apple.

SCAMPER: I'm sure glad you followed me to the park!

SCOUT: There you were, *(points upward)* up in that orange tree—

SCAMPER: *(interrupts)* Apple tree, Scout! It was an apple tree!

SCOUT: Whatever. I don't like fruit, so I didn't really notice.

SCAMPER: There were lots of trees, weren't there?

SCOUT: There were all kinds of trees. How many kinds did you see?

SCAMPER: I think a kazillion! *(spreads paws)* Some of them had fruit.

SCOUT: Squirrels must like fruit.

SCAMPER: I do! I picked the biggest apple I could find.

SCOUT: Funny Scamper. *(giggles)* That apple was almost as big as you.

SCAMPER: No wonder I dropped it.

SCOUT: *(giggles)* Right into a big pile of leaves!

SCAMPER: I thought I'd lost it.

SCOUT: You scrambled through those leaves, looking for the apple!

SCAMPER: I'm glad you were there, Scout.

SCOUT: *(proudly)* I found the apple, didn't I?

SCAMPER: It was funny, Scout! *(giggles)* You uncovered my apple with your tail!

SCOUT: I was just wagging.

SCAMPER: You wagged in the right place. Those leaves scattered!

SCOUT: I'm glad I found your apple, Scamper.

SCAMPER: Me too! It was delicious! I even brought one home to eat later! *(picks up apple in paws and holds through end of script)*

SCOUT: It's good that people take care of gardens and parks.

SCAMPER: They use their hands to pick fruit and vegetables.

SCOUT: You use your mouth and paws.

SCAMPER: I hold food with my paws when I eat.

SCOUT: The caretaker used a rake to move leaves.

SCAMPER: *(giggles)* You used your tail!

SCOUT: *(giggles)*

SCAMPER: We use our bodies to do different things.

SCOUT: God made our bodies special. And He made peoples' bodies special too!

SCAMPER: God thought of everything!

Discussion Questions

1. What does Scamper use to hold his food?
2. How did Scout use his tail?
3. What do you think Adam used his legs to do?
4. What do you think Eve used her hands to do?
5. What fruit can you pick with your hands?
6. What do you use your feet to do?

God Made People Special

Based on: Genesis 1, 2; Proverbs 20—God Made My Senses
Props: none

SCAMPER:	Hi, Scout!
SCOUT:	Hi. You seem happy today.
SCAMPER:	I am happy. *(looks at children)* I get to see my friends in this class.
SCOUT:	*(looks at children)* Our friends look good. I like the bright colors they wear.
SCAMPER:	I'm glad I can see.
SCOUT:	The children sing happy songs. I'm glad I can hear.
SCAMPER:	Birds sing too, Scout. I like to hear them.
SCOUT:	What else can we hear, Scamper?
SCAMPER:	Rain. I like to hear rain splashing on the leaves.
SCOUT:	I stick my tongue out to taste the rain!
SCAMPER:	Fresh water does taste good!
SCOUT:	Puppy Crunch tastes good too!
SCAMPER:	Yuk! I don't like dog food!
SCOUT:	What tastes good to you, Scamper?
SCAMPER:	I like acorns and corn. I sometimes eat fruit.
SCOUT:	You might like Puppy Crunch if you tasted it.
SCAMPER:	I don't want to.
SCOUT:	Why, Scamper? Why won't you just try it?

SCAMPER:	Puppy Crunch smells bad. That's why I won't taste it.
SCOUT:	To me, it smells delicious!
SCAMPER:	I like to smell peanut butter!
SCOUT:	Me too. Sometimes my girl shares her peanut butter sandwich with me.
SCAMPER:	Seedcakes are made with peanut butter. The birds and I share too.
SCOUT:	It must be almost lunchtime.
SCAMPER:	I think so, Scout. My stomach feels hungry.
SCOUT:	*(feels Scamper's stomach with paw)* You don't feel hungry to me.
SCAMPER:	*(giggles)* Funny Scout! I feel hungry inside! You are feeling outside.
SCOUT:	Oh. *(giggles)* That is funny! *(pauses)* Your fur feels soft.
SCAMPER:	*(looks at stomach)* I am soft.
SCOUT:	God made us able to taste and smell.
SCAMPER:	He gave us ears so we can hear.
SCOUT:	We can see with our eyes.
SCAMPER:	Can people do all those things too?
SCOUT:	*(nods)* Yes.
SCAMPER:	God made people special.

Discussion Questions

1. What does Scamper like to hear?
2. What food does Scout like?
3. How did Adam use his hands in the garden?
4. What do you think Eve heard in the garden? (saw?)
5. What body part do you use to taste things? (smell?)
6. What animal would you like to pet?

God Made Each of Us Special

Based on: Genesis 1, 2; Psalms 8, 139; Matthew 10—God Made Me Special
Props: Scout should be holding a stick at the start of the script.

SCAMPER: Wow, Scout! I saw you catch that stick in your mouth!

SCOUT: Yep. I learned to do that yesterday.

SCAMPER: You are smart and strong.

SCOUT: *(proudly)* I can jump high and catch.

SCOUT: That's OK, you can do things I can't do.

SCAMPER: *(skeptical)* Are you sure?

SCOUT: *(sternly)* I can't climb trees, remember?

SCAMPER: *(happily)* Oh yeah. *(giggles)* I forgot.

SCOUT: We are not alike at all.

SCAMPER: You live in a house and I live in a tree nest.

SCOUT: You are reddish brown, and I am white and brown.

SCAMPER: *(looks at stomach)* I have some white too.

SCOUT: *(holds paw next to Scamper's stomach)* Our white fur looks the same!

SCAMPER: We are alike and different!

SCOUT: Let's tell what is the same and different about us.

SCAMPER: That sounds like fun!

SCOUT: Alike first. We both like to play.

SCAMPER: I know what is different. We eat different foods.

SCOUT: That's right. You eat acorns and I eat Puppy Crunch!

SCAMPER: What else is alike?

SCOUT: We both have four feet!

SCAMPER: And we both have tails!

SCOUT: Both of us having tails is alike.

SCAMPER: But our tails look different. *(giggles)* Yours is small and mine is bushy.

SCOUT: *(giggles)* You're right, Scamper! *(looks at Scamper's tail)*

SCAMPER: I know what is different! You bark and I chatter.

SCOUT: God made each of us special.

SCAMPER: We look different.

SCOUT: We have different homes.

SCAMPER: But do you know what else is the same?

SCOUT: What?

SCAMPER: We both love each other.

SCOUT: We are forever friends. *(Scout and Scamper hug each other)*

Discussion Questions

1. How are Scout and Scamper different?
2. How are Scout and Scamper the same?
3. Who gave names to all the animals?
4. Who knew you before you were born?
5. What color is your hair?
6. What do you like most about how God made you?

God Wants Us to Obey Him

Based on: Genesis 6, 7—Noah Builds a Boat
Props: none

SCAMPER: Scout, where are you?

SCOUT: *(out of sight)* Over here, Scamper!

SCAMPER: Come and play!

SCOUT: I can't. Not yet!

SCAMPER: *(to himself)* I wonder what Scout is doing?

SCOUT: *(arrives, panting)* I tried to hurry, Scamper.

SCAMPER: Where were you?

SCOUT: I was at my house.

SCAMPER: Why didn't you come when I called?

SCOUT: My girl told me to sit and stay.

SCAMPER: *(questioning, holds up both paws)* What does that mean?

SCOUT: It means I am supposed to sit and not leave until she says I can. I'm a good dog. I obey my people.

SCAMPER: Oh, I see.

SCOUT: After I sit a little while, she gives me a Puppy Crunch Bone. Then I can run and play.

SCAMPER: Sometimes I have to sit still too.

SCOUT: You do? Who tells you to sit?

SCAMPER: No one says anything. Squirrels give a signal.

SCOUT: What is a signal?

SCAMPER: If a squirrel sees danger, the signal is tail wiggling.

SCOUT: *(giggles)* Is that like a dog's tail wagging?

SCAMPER: Almost, but it is quicker, *(turns around to show tail)* like this! *(shakes tail sharply 4 or 5 times)*

SCOUT: That is a good signal, Scamper!

SCAMPER: All the little squirrels obey and stay very still until the danger is past.

SCOUT: It is very important for little squirrels to obey.

SCAMPER: They might be in danger if they don't obey.

SCOUT: My people teach me to obey so I won't get into trouble.

SCAMPER: God was the first to teach people to obey.

SCOUT: So people must obey too?

SCAMPER: Yep. God has rules for people too. God wants them to obey Him.

SCOUT: I'm going to always obey my people!

SCAMPER: Good dog, Scout! I'll obey too.

Discussion Questions

1. How is Scout a good dog?
2. What signal does Scamper obey?
3. How did Noah obey God?
4. Who got to ride in the ark?
5. Who should you obey?
6. How can you obey?

God Cares for Us

Based on: Genesis 7–9—Noah and the Flood
Props: none

SCAMPER: *(wipes eyes) Sniff. Boo-hoo.*

SCOUT: What's wrong, Scamper?

SCAMPER: *(sadly)* I am not happy. *(sighs)* No one cares about me.

SCOUT: I do! I care about you a lot! *(hugs Scamper)*

SCAMPER: Sniff. Thank you, Scout!

SCOUT: What happened?

SCAMPER: The other squirrels won't play with me.

SCOUT: Aw, sure they will.

SCAMPER: No they won't. They all ran away from me.

SCOUT: Maybe they didn't mean to be unkind.

SCAMPER: They were laughing.

SCOUT: Don't worry, Scamper. *(pats Scamper)* I'm your forever friend. I'll play with you.

SCAMPER: Thank you, Scout. *(sniff)* I know you love me. You are my only friend.

SCOUT: Someone else cares too.

SCAMPER: Really? Who is it?

SCOUT: God.

SCAMPER: He does? How do you know?

SCOUT: The Bible says God made all the animals. God cares for us.

SCAMPER: I'm glad God cares.

SCOUT: Why did your friends run away?

SCAMPER: *(hangs head)* I don't know. They just shouted that I was *it* and hurried away! *(pauses)* Scout, I'm not an *it*, am I?

SCOUT: *(giggles and pats Scamper)* Oh, Scamper! You don't understand.

SCAMPER: *(looks up)* I sure don't!

SCOUT: They just want to play a game with you.

SCAMPER: I don't think that game is nice!

SCOUT: You will when you understand. The game is called tag.

SCAMPER: I don't know how to play.

SCOUT: It's easy to play. If you are *it,* you chase everyone. Whoever you catch becomes it and tries to catch another squirrel.

SCAMPER: *(cheerfully)* That sounds like fun!

SCOUT: I knew you would like the game.

SCAMPER: I'm going to catch up with them! I'm fast and can tag someone quickly. Bye, Scout!

SCOUT: See you later, Scamper.

Discussion Questions

1. Why did the other squirrels run away?
2. Who made all animals and people?
3. What was Noah's big boat called?
4. How did God care for Noah and the animals during the flood?
5. How has God cared for you?
6. How can you thank God?

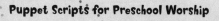

God Wants Us to Follow Him

Based on: Genesis 12—Abram Moves
Props: none

SCOUT: Scamper, let's play follow the leader!

SCAMPER: (scratches his head) I don't know how.

SCOUT: It's easy. I'll be the leader first.

SCAMPER: OK.

SCOUT: When I run, you must run behind me.

SCAMPER: I can do that.

SCOUT: If I jump over something, you jump over it too.

SCAMPER: I can do that.

SCOUT: When I crawl under something, you have to follow.

SCAMPER: OK, Scout, I get it! I'll follow you everywhere and do exactly what you do.

SCOUT: Here goes! (taps front paws together)

SCAMPER: (taps front paws together) I can do it too!

SCOUT: Try this! (turns and walks away from Scamper)

SCAMPER: (turns and follows Scout) Easy.

SCOUT: (turns to Scamper and hides eyes)

SCAMPER: (hides eyes)

SCOUT: (removes paws from eyes)

SCAMPER: (peeks from behind one paw, then the other) No fair! I couldn't see what you were doing!

SCOUT: OK, it's your turn to be leader.

SCAMPER: This is going to be fun! (rubs front paws together)

SCOUT: (rubs front paws together) I can do that!

SCAMPER: Try this. (waves at children)

SCOUT: (waves at children) Think of something harder.

SCAMPER: OK. (holds left paw against stomach, then reaches right paw forward and sings) Put your right paw in. (places right paw against stomach) Pull your right paw out (places right paw forward, and shake it all about! (shakes right paw)

SCOUT: (Scout speaks slowly, confused) Let's see, now. Put your right paw out. (reaches both paws forward) Put your left paw in. (places both paws on stomach) Shake all about! (shakes entire body)

SCAMPER: (giggles) Oh Scout! You are funny!

SCOUT: (giggles) I give up. I can't follow you.

SCAMPER: I know someone we can follow.

SCOUT: Who?

SCAMPER: God. God wants us to follow Him.

Discussion Questions

1. What game did Scout want to play?
2. Who didn't know right paw from left paw?
3. Who followed God when God asked him to?
4. Who went with Abram?
5. Have you ever moved to a new house?
6. How do you feel about going to new places?

God Wants Us to Make Good Choices

Based on: Genesis 13—Abram and Lot
Props: Place a small ball next to Scout, and tie a blown-up balloon with a string to Scamper's paw.

SCAMPER: We are having such fun with our new toys! *(jerks arm to make balloon bounce)* Wheee!

SCOUT: Yeah, I love my new ball. *(touches ball with one paw)*

SCAMPER: I'm glad the Woodsy Toy Shop had balloons. I love balloons!

SCOUT: *(nods)* There were so many choices to make!

SCAMPER: I almost got a swing to hang from my tree. That would have been fun.

SCOUT: I saw a stuffed doggie toy I liked.

SCAMPER: It is hard to pick just one toy.

SCOUT: It's really hard, Scamper.

SCAMPER: I'm going to fly my balloon from my tree. It will blow in the breeze.

SCOUT: That color will look good with the fall leaves.

SCAMPER: *Wheee! (bounces balloon with paw)* I will sit on the limb and bounce with my balloon!

SCOUT: OK. I will stand on the ground and watch.

SCAMPER: I'll do it right now. Get ready to watch me, Scout!

(Scamper disappears out of sight while teacher removes the balloon from Scamper's paw. Scamper returns a moment later.)

SCAMPER: Oh no! Did you see my beautiful balloon? I lost hold of it and it floated up in the sky. *(places paws over eyes as though crying)*

SCOUT: Don't cry, Scamper. *(pats Scamper)* You can play with my ball.

SCAMPER: Why did I choose a balloon? Now it's gone.

SCOUT: Next time, you can pick a different toy.

SCAMPER: I sure will. I will think about it and choose something that will not break so easily.

SCOUT: *(picks up ball with front paws)* Here, Scamper. You can play with my ball. *(places ball in front of Scamper)*

SCAMPER: *(picks up ball)* Thank you, Scout.

SCOUT: I'm glad we can share.

SCAMPER: Me too, Scout. You are my friend.

Discussion Questions

1. What toy did Scout buy?
2. What happened to Scamper's toy?
3. What did Abram and Lot choose?
4. Which one chose selfishly?
5. If there were two cookies, would you let your friend choose first?
6. Who can help you make good choices?

 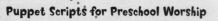

God Cares for Families

Based on: Genesis 17, 18, 21—Abraham and Sarah Have a Baby
Props: none

Scout:	*(excited)* I have big news, Scamper!
Scamper:	What is it, Scout?
Scout:	A new baby lives at our house!
Scamper:	A puppy?
Scout:	No, not a puppy.
Scamper:	*(hopefully)* A squirrel, like me? *(points to self)*
Scout:	Not a squirrel.
Scamper:	What else is there? Tell me!
Scout:	It is a person.
Scamper:	Oh, I understand now. It is one of your people.
Scout:	You guessed it!
Scamper:	Is it a boy person or a girl person?
Scout:	It is a boy. Now I can play with a girl and a boy.
Scamper:	That will be fun.
Scout:	*(longingly)* I can't wait until he is big enough to walk and play.
Scamper:	*(unbelievingly)* He can't walk?
Scout:	Not yet.
Scamper:	Baby squirrels can walk in just a few days.
Scout:	So can dogs, but people babies have to grow first.
Scamper:	*(confused)* That is weird!
Scout:	It may seem strange to you, but that's how God planned it. I like my family.
Scamper:	How many are in your family now?
Scout:	Let me count. *(scratches head and thinks)* The father, the mother, and the little girl, um . . . are there two people?
Scamper:	*(giggles)* No Scout. Count again; one, two, three.
Scout:	That's right, three.
Scamper:	The baby makes one more. What number comes after three?
Scout:	Four.
Scamper:	*(pats Scout)* Good dog! That's right!
Scout:	You forgot one family member.
Scamper:	I did? Who?
Scout:	*(giggles)* Funny Scamper! You forgot to count *(points to self)* me!
Scamper:	Oops, sorry, Scout! Another one comes to five; five in the family!
Scout:	I'm happy to be part of a family.
Scamper:	God cares for families.
Scout:	I know.

Discussion Questions

1. What was Scout's big news?
2. How many are in Scout's family?
3. What promise did God give to Abraham and Sarah?
4. Was their baby a boy or a girl?
5. How many people are in your family?
6. Who cares for families?

God Cares for Us All the Time

Based on: Genesis 37, 39—Joseph as a Boy
Props: none

SCAMPER: That was a big storm last night, wasn't it?

SCOUT: *(shivers)* It sure was! I was afraid!

SCAMPER: *(turns to Scout, questioningly)* Why?

SCOUT: The wind was blowing very hard!

SCAMPER: I know. *(rocks back and forth)* It rocked my tree and put me to sleep.

SCOUT: Did you see the lightning? *(covers eyes)*

SCAMPER: Yep. It was cool, just like fireworks on the Fourth of July! *(emphatically raises paw twice)* Flash! Pow!

SCOUT: Did you hear the hail?

SCAMPER: Uh-huh, I did. It knocked some nuts off my tree! Now I don't have to carry them down to the ground to bury them.

SCOUT: The hail went *bang, bang, bang* on our roof!

SCAMPER: I like to see it bounce on the ground. It looked almost like snow.

SCOUT: *(holds ears)* The thunder was so loud!

SCAMPER: *(reassuringly)* Thunder can't hurt you. Besides, God is with you—even in the storm. *(pats Scout)*

SCOUT: *(wonderingly)* I didn't know that.

SCAMPER: God cares for us all the time.

SCOUT: Even when we are afraid?

SCAMPER: Even when it storms, He is there. God is with us anytime we are afraid.

SCOUT: I'm glad to hear that!

SCAMPER: Hey, Scout, let's play a game next time it storms.

SCOUT: I'm not going out in any storm to play!

SCAMPER: *(giggles)* Me either. We can play in our homes.

SCOUT: OK.

SCAMPER: We will count the flashes of lightning.

SCOUT: What if I have my eyes closed?

SCAMPER: If your eyes are closed, you won't see the night sky light up. God will help you to be brave.

SCOUT: OK, I can look and count because God is with me in the storm.

Discussion Questions

1. How did Scout feel about the storm?
2. Why wasn't Scamper afraid?
3. What happened to Joseph?
4. Who helped Joseph to be brave?
5. When are you afraid?
6. Who can help you to be brave?

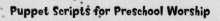

God Wants Us to Serve Him

Based on: Genesis 39, 41, 42, 45, 47—Joseph Serves God All His Life
Props: Place a large acorn behind Scout. Scamper should be wrapped in a baby blanket.

SCAMPER: *(sadly)* Hi, Scout.

SCOUT: Hi, Scamper. Are you ready to play?

SCAMPER: No.

SCOUT: Why can't you play? Do you have to do chores for your mother?

SCAMPER: No. I feel badly. *(softly)* I have a fever.

SCOUT: I'm sorry, Scamper. It's no fun to be sick!

SCAMPER: Nope. My mother made me take medicine.

SCOUT: That's too bad.

SCAMPER: She says I have to stay in bed.

SCOUT: That's no fun.

SCAMPER: I don't feel like going outside anyway. I think I'll take a nap.

SCOUT: OK, Scamper. You get some rest. I'll wait for you to feel better.

SCAMPER: *(leans against teacher and snuggles under blanket so eyes are not visible)*

SCOUT: *(whispers to children)* Shhh. I think Scamper is asleep now.

SCAMPER: *(makes soft snoring sounds)*

SCOUT: I wonder what I could do for a surprise. I want to help Scamper feel better. *(scratches head, thinking)* I know! I'll find an acorn for Scamper! *(looks around and sees acorn)* Here's one!

SCAMPER: *(snoring softly)*

SCOUT: *(picks up acorn and walks to Scamper)* I'd better tiptoe, so I don't wake Scamper.

SCAMPER: *(snores softly, wriggles, then peeks from under blanket)* Are you still here, Scout?

SCOUT: Yes. I brought you something to help you feel better. *(lays acorn next to Scamper)*

SCAMPER: *(looks at acorn, then at Scout)* Oh, thank you, Scout! I love acorns!

SCOUT: You're welcome.

SCAMPER: You pleased me today, and you pleased God.

SCOUT: I did? How?

SCAMPER: God wants us to serve others. You served me, and that makes God happy.

SCOUT: I was just showing my love for my best friend.

SCAMPER: I feel better knowing I am loved.

Discussion Questions

1. What is wrong with Scamper today?
2. What did Scout do to help Scamper feel better?
3. How did Joseph serve in Egypt?
4. What was the king of Egypt called?
5. Has anyone ever served you? Who?
6. How could you serve a friend?

God Cares for Us Everywhere We Go

Based on: Exodus 2—Moses Is Born
Props: none

SCAMPER: Scout, I've been looking for you!

SCOUT: *(yawns)* I was hiding.

SCAMPER: You weren't in your doghouse.

SCOUT: Nope.

SCAMPER: You weren't under the porch.

SCOUT: Nope. *(stretches front legs upward while yawning)*

SCAMPER: You weren't under your favorite shade tree.

SCOUT: Nope.

SCAMPER: I give up. Where were you?

SCOUT: I was in the house, under a bed.

SCAMPER: Why?

SCOUT: I played and played until I was tired. I wanted a nap.

SCAMPER: Why didn't you sleep *(emphasizes)* on the bed?

SCOUT: I'm not allowed on the beds. Anyway, I didn't want to be found.

SCAMPER: You'd have been found if you were on top of the bed, all right.

SCOUT: I had a good nap.

SCAMPER: Hiding is fun. I hide nuts in the ground.

SCOUT: Why?

SCAMPER: To keep them safe until I am hungry. Then I dig them up and eat them.

SCOUT: I do that with bones. I save them for later.

SCAMPER: *(looks at children)* Do you all hide things? *(allow answers from children)*

SCOUT: They hide things, just like we do, Scamper!

SCAMPER: *(giggles)* They must have good hiding places!

SCOUT: *(looks at children)* Do you ever play hide-and-seek? *(allow answers from children)*

SCAMPER: I love to play hide-and-seek!

SCOUT: I like to hide so well that no one can find me.

SCAMPER: There is someone who always knows where you are, Scout.

SCOUT: Who?

SCAMPER: God.

SCOUT: Does He peek when we hide?

SCAMPER: God doesn't have to peek. He knows everything.

SCOUT: Does He always know where the children are?

SCAMPER: Always. God cares for us everywhere we go.

SCOUT: Let's play hide-and-seek now!

Discussion Questions

1. Where did Scout hide?
2. Why does Scamper hide nuts?
3. Where did the princess find baby Moses?
4. Who took care of baby Moses?
5. Who takes care of you?
6. Where is your favorite place to hide?

God Is Always with Us

Based on: Exodus 3, 7–13—Moses Leads God's People
Props: none

SCAMPER: Hi, Scout!

SCOUT: Hi! I'm a little bit cold today.

SCAMPER: So am I, Scout.

SCOUT: If I get too cold, I just go into the house to get warm.

SCAMPER: I go into my nest.

SCOUT: The furnace keeps our house warm.

SCAMPER: My nest is not heated.

SCOUT: You will freeze when winter comes!

SCAMPER: No I won't.

SCOUT: What if it snows?

SCAMPER: I'll be snug and warm in my new coat.

SCOUT: You're getting a new coat?

SCAMPER: Yep. Outdoor animals grow a new, warmer coat each winter.

SCOUT: How do you grow a coat?

SCAMPER: *(giggles)* It is my fur, Scout. *(holds out arm)* See how much thicker my coat of fur is getting?

SCOUT: *(feels Scamper's fur with paw)* It *(emphasizes) is* getting thicker!

SCAMPER: *(rubs face with paw)* It's pretty, don't you think?

SCOUT: Very pretty.

SCAMPER: Thank you. Your fur is nice too.

SCOUT: Is it getting thick, like yours?

SCAMPER: *(feels Scout's arm)* You are growing a new coat too!

SCOUT: *(rubs stomach with paw)* You're right, Scamper. I can feel it!

SCAMPER: It will be warm.

SCOUT: *(excited)* Hey, Scamper, do the children grow their coats?

SCAMPER: *(giggles)* Funny Scout! Their families buy coats for them!

SCOUT: What makes animals grow new fur?

SCAMPER: God planned it that way.

SCOUT: I guess He knew we couldn't go to the store and buy a coat.

SCAMPER: *(giggles)* Animals have no money. They don't go to the store.

SCOUT: Animals can't get new coats by themselves.

SCAMPER: God does it for them. He makes their fur grow thick and warm.

SCOUT: God is always with us.

SCAMPER: He helps with things we can't do ourselves.

SCOUT: He loves and helps people everywhere.

Discussion Questions

1. Who grew a winter coat?
2. What keeps animals warm in winter?
3. How did God help His people in Egypt?
4. Who was the leader of the people?
5. When do you ask for God's help?
6. How has God helped you?

God Helps Us When We Are Afraid

Based on: Exodus 13–15—God's People Cross the Red Sea

Props: Set a small spray bottle nearby. When Scout pretends to shake water off of his fur at the beginning of the script, spray a small amount of water in the air so that it appears that Scout is really wet.

SCOUT: *(shakes off pretend water)*

SCAMPER: *(wipes face with paws)* Hey, you got me wet!

SCOUT: Oops, sorry, Scamper.

SCAMPER: It's OK. I wiped it off.

SCOUT: You should have been there!

SCAMPER: Were you playing in the pond again?

SCOUT: *(happily)* Yep. It was fun!

SCAMPER: I don't like the pond.

SCOUT: Why?

SCAMPER: I am afraid of so much water!

SCOUT: You can't live without water, Scamper!

SCAMPER: I know. I get my water from the birdbath.

SCOUT: It has only a little bit of water.

SCAMPER: I know. It is enough for me.

SCOUT: I like lots of water. It's fun to get wet!

SCAMPER: Did you go alone to the pond?

SCOUT: I'm not allowed to go alone.

SCAMPER: Who goes with you?

SCOUT: My people take me there. They throw a stick into the water.

SCAMPER: Why?

SCOUT: It is a game. I swim out to get the stick and bring it back.

SCAMPER: I guess it is fun if you aren't afraid of the water.

SCOUT: *(happily)* It is lots of fun!

SCAMPER: *(looks at children)* Do children play in water?

SCOUT: I think they all play in the bathtub.

SCAMPER: I mean big water! Big water like at the pond.

SCOUT: Some do.

SCAMPER: Am I the only one who is afraid?

SCOUT: Sometimes children are afraid at the lake or the ocean.

SCAMPER: That's too bad. It's no fun to be afraid.

SCOUT: God helps us when we are afraid.

SCAMPER: *(happily)* I'm glad God watches over us all.

SCOUT: God loves the children, *(pauses)* and animals too!

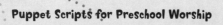

Discussion Questions

1. What did Scout do at the lake?
2. Where is the water that Scamper likes?
3. How did Moses and the people get past the water?
4. How did Moses and the people praise God?
5. What frightens you?
6. For what do you thank God?

Puppet Scripts for Preschool Worship

God Gives Us What We Need

Based on: Exodus 16, 17—God Provides for His People
Props: Scatter some cereal nearby—a nut and grain mixture.

SCAMPER: *(excited)* Hey, Scout! I want to tell you something!

SCOUT: What is it, Scamper?

SCAMPER: I have a new favorite food!

SCOUT: I thought your favorite was acorns.

SCAMPER: It was until today.

SCOUT: What is your new favorite food?

SCAMPER: I don't know what it is called. I just know it is yummy!

SCOUT: Where did you get the new food?

SCAMPER: In your yard! It was scattered everywhere!

SCOUT: Now I know what it is.

SCAMPER: You do? What is it?

SCOUT: It is Cinnamon Nutty Os cereal.

SCAMPER: What is it made of?

SCOUT: Nuts and grains.

SCAMPER: No wonder it is so good. I like nuts and grains.

SCOUT: My people threw it out there for the birds.

SCAMPER: The birds and I had breakfast together. They shared with me.

SCOUT: That's nice.

SCAMPER: There was plenty for all of us. We ate until we were full.

SCOUT: You and the birds must have been hungry. There was a lot of cereal out there.

SCAMPER: We were. It was exactly enough.

SCOUT: My people like to take care of animals and birds.

SCAMPER: They know what we need.

SCOUT: *(looks at children)* What do the children need?

SCAMPER: They need food, clothes, and a place to live.

SCOUT: Their families give them what they need.

SCAMPER: And God too.

SCOUT: God?

SCAMPER: Yes. God gives us all what we need.

SCOUT: How can He do that?

SCAMPER: He uses other people.

SCOUT: People, like families and teachers?

SCAMPER: Yep.

SCOUT: I guess he used my people to feed you and the birds today.

SCAMPER: Yummy!

Discussion Questions

1. Where do birds get their food?
2. What does Scamper like to eat?
3. Where did the Israelites find their food?
4. How much food did they gather each day?
5. Where do you get your food?
6. What is your favorite food?

God Gives Us Good Rules to Obey

Based on: Exodus 19, 20, 24, 32—God Gives Ten Rules
Props: none

SCOUT: Hi, Scamper!

SCAMPER: What's up, Scout?

SCOUT: I'm in training.

SCAMPER: What are you in training for?

SCOUT: I'm learning to be a good dog in the house.

SCAMPER: You are always good, Scout.

SCOUT: I know, but there are rules I must obey.

SCAMPER: What kind of rules?

SCOUT: I can't get on the sofa or chairs.

SCAMPER: People sit on furniture. Why can't you?

SCOUT: Because I shed hair. It gets all over everything.

SCAMPER: What's wrong with that?

SCOUT: It has to be clean, so my hair doesn't get on their clothes.

SCAMPER: Oh. I guess it wouldn't look good if they came to church with dog hair all over their Sunday outfits.

SCOUT: *(giggles)* I guess not.

SCAMPER: What other rules do you have to obey?

SCOUT: I can't bark a lot.

SCAMPER: Why not?

SCOUT: If the baby is asleep, it might wake him.

SCAMPER: If someone is talking on the phone, you need to be quiet.

SCOUT: That too.

SCAMPER: Are there more rules?

SCOUT: Yep. No jumping on people. That's the first one I learned.

SCAMPER: But you do that because you are happy to see them.

SCOUT: If I have muddy feet, it would get them all dirty.

SCAMPER: That's a good reason.

SCOUT: There are reasons for every rule.

SCAMPER: It is good that you are in training. You can learn to obey.

SCOUT: *(looks at children)* The children have rules to obey too.

SCAMPER: God gives us good rules to obey.

SCOUT: They are learning too.

SCAMPER: Their families and teachers teach them.

SCOUT: They can learn to obey and please God.

Discussion Questions

1. Who makes rules for Scout?
2. What is one of Scout's rules?
3. How many rules did God give to Moses?
4. Where did Moses go to get the rules?
5. Who makes rules for you?
6. Where can we read God's rules?

God Is Powerful—He Will Help Us

Based on: Numbers 13, 14—Joshua and Caleb

Props: Set several kinds of nuts nearby. Scamper mentions walnuts, hickory nuts, and acorns in this script, so collect these if possible.

SCAMPER: Hey, Scout, guess where I've been.

SCOUT: Um, did you go to the zoo?

SCAMPER: No.

SCOUT: Did you go to town?

SCAMPER: Nope!

SCOUT: *(puzzled)* Where did you go?

SCAMPER: I went to the woods.

SCOUT: Why?

SCAMPER: To explore!

SCOUT: That sounds like fun. What did you find there?

SCAMPER: I found the best nut trees! There were *(gesturing to a pile of nuts nearby)* walnuts, hickory nuts, and acorns!

SCOUT: You'll be busy picking and hiding nuts for winter.

SCAMPER: I sure will.

SCOUT: What else did you see?

SCAMPER: I saw some funny animals near a pond.

SCOUT: What did they look like?

SCAMPER: They were dark brown and were chewing on trees.

SCOUT: They must have been beavers. Beavers cut down trees with their teeth.

SCAMPER: Awesome! *(giggles)* They don't even need chain saws!

SCOUT: What else was in the woods?

SCAMPER: I saw birds.

SCOUT: What kinds of birds?

SCAMPER: One had long legs and was catching fish to eat in the pond.

SCOUT: I've seen that bird in my pond. He is tall!

SCAMPER: Other birds were floating on the water.

SCOUT: Those are ducks.

SCAMPER: Baby ducks were floating behind their mother.

SCOUT: Did you play in the water with them?

SCAMPER: *(sternly)* Scout, you know I don't like the water!

SCOUT: *(giggles)* I know. I just wanted to tease you.

SCAMPER: We could explore together in the woods. I could take you there. I know the way.

SCOUT: OK, Scamper. We'll go tomorrow.

SCAMPER: It's fun to explore!

SCOUT: What if I don't remember the way back?

SCAMPER: God is powerful. He will help us.

SCOUT: Will you know the way home, Scamper?

SCAMPER: God gives squirrels the ability to remember how to get home.

SCOUT: See you tomorrow, Scamper!

Discussion Questions

1. Where did Scamper explore?
2. What did Scamper find in the woods?
3. Who went to Canaan to explore?
4. What kind of people lived in Canaan?
5. Where do you explore?
6. What good things have you found?

God Is Powerful—He Is with Us

Based on: Joshua 1, 3, 4—God's People Cross the Jordan River
Props: none

SCOUT: I had fun yesterday.

SCAMPER: I saw you get into the car with your people.

SCOUT: We went for a drive.

SCAMPER: Where did you go?

SCOUT: We crossed the river into the next state!

SCAMPER: Oh. Did you go on a big bridge?

SCOUT: No.

SCAMPER: Scout, there has to be a bridge!

SCOUT: There was no bridge.

SCAMPER: You can't just drive across the water!

SCOUT: We went on a ferry boat!

SCAMPER: I don't know what a ferry boat is.

SCOUT: I didn't either. It was the first one I had seen.

SCAMPER: What was it like?

SCOUT: A big, flat boat was in the water. It had a ramp going to the land.

SCAMPER: Did you walk up the ramp?

SCOUT: No. We drove on it to get onto the boat!

SCAMPER: Wow! That is cool!

SCOUT: It was! We rode on the boat to the other side!

SCAMPER: In the car?

SCOUT: We got out of the car and stood by the railing.

SCAMPER: Were you afraid of the water?

SCOUT: No. It was fun.

SCAMPER: Were there lots of cars?

SCOUT: There were about 10 cars.

SCAMPER: That sounds like a powerful boat!

SCOUT: It was. It carried all the people and cars to the other side. *(pauses)* You know, God made the water.

SCAMPER: Yes, and He can control the water.

SCOUT: God is powerful. He is with us.

SCAMPER: I'm glad, Scout.

SCOUT: Me too.

SCAMPER: Do you want to play awhile?

SCOUT: *(excited)* Oh yes! Let's go to my yard. We can play with my ball.

SCAMPER: Let's go!

Discussion Questions

1. On what kind of boat did Scout ride?
2. What did Scout do on the boat?
3. How did Joshua and the people cross the river?
4. Why did the people make a pile of rocks after they crossed the river?
5. Have you ever ridden on a boat?
6. Who is more powerful than the water?

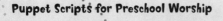

God Is Powerful—We Should Obey Him

Based on: Joshua 6—The Fall of Jericho
Props: Bring a small toy drum and drumstick to class. You may substitute another parade instrument that is played by striking.

SCOUT: *(holds drumstick and strikes drum repeatedly—if puppet cannot attain a strong volume, have someone out of sight strike another instrument at the appropriate time)*

SCAMPER: *(pops up, holding ears)* Hey, what's all the noise? Can't you be quiet?

SCOUT: *(quits striking drum)* Scamper, I'm having fun! Listen to this! *(begins to beat drum)*

SCAMPER: *(covers ears)* That is loud!

SCOUT: *(quits beating drum)* There is a reason drums are loud.

SCAMPER: Why?

SCOUT: They are used in parades. Everyone in the parade must hear and march to the music.

SCAMPER: How do they march to the music?

SCOUT: Easy. Take one step each time I strike the drum. That is called marching.

SCAMPER: Let's try it! You play the drum and I'll march.

SCOUT: *(plays a steady beat)* Go, Scamper! *(continues for four to six beats while Scamper marches)*

SCAMPER: *(marches with a steady up and down movement in time to the beat)* You were a good leader. I followed you.

SCOUT: The children can follow God's leading.

SCAMPER: Is God having a parade?

SCOUT: *(giggles)* Silly Scamper.

SCAMPER: How can the children follow God?

SCOUT: He tells us how to follow Him. He is a good leader.

SCAMPER: You mean in the Bible?

SCOUT: Yep. Here is how we follow Him. *(strikes drum and rhythmically chants)* God is love. *(pauses and Scamper begins marching)* Love one another. *(pause)* Obey God.

SCAMPER: *(giggles and claps paws)* I can march to the beat!

SCOUT: See? That's how we can follow God.

SCAMPER: God is powerful. We should obey Him.

SCOUT: *(beats a steady rhythm as puppets march away)*

Discussion Questions

1. What instrument was Scout playing?
2. What important book tells us how to follow God?
3. How did Joshua and the people travel around Jericho?
4. What instrument did the priests blow?
5. Can you play an instrument? march?
6. Who do you obey?

God Is Powerful—We Can Serve Him

Based on: Joshua 24—Joshua Talks to God's People
Props: Set a few pieces of wadded-up paper and a small trash can nearby.

SCAMPER: *(looks at paper wads)* Hey, Scout! Look at this mess!

SCOUT: Yuk! That makes our classroom look bad.

SCAMPER: I wonder who left that paper here?

SCOUT: I don't know.

SCAMPER: Someone should clean it up.

SCOUT: Not me! I didn't do it!

SCAMPER: I didn't do it, either.

SCOUT: Why do people throw trash around?

SCAMPER: I wonder why they don't just put it into a trash can.

SCOUT: Someone threw stuff from a car onto our yard last week.

SCAMPER: Why?

SCOUT: That's what I'd like to know.

SCAMPER: They should put it in a litterbag.

SCOUT: Maybe they didn't have one.

SCAMPER: There is still another choice.

SCOUT: Really?

SCAMPER: Sure. They could save it until they come to a roadside trash can.

SCOUT: My family had to clean it up.

SCAMPER: They did?

SCOUT: *(looks at paper wads)* If I knew who did it, I'd make them clean it up!

SCAMPER: We have another choice.

SCOUT: We do?

SCAMPER: We could clean it up.

SCOUT: Uh-uh. We didn't make the mess!

SCAMPER: We can do it for the church.

SCOUT: OK, Scamper. We will do it for God.

SCAMPER: The children help sometimes. We can too.

SCOUT: God is pleased when someone chooses to do good things.

SCAMPER: God is powerful.

SCOUT: We can serve Him.

SCAMPER: I choose to help. *(picks up a paper wad and drops it into trash can)*

SCOUT: I can do it too! *(picks up a paper wad and drops it into trash can)*

(Scout and Scamper continue to pick up paper wads until all are in trash)

SCAMPER: High five! *(Scout and Scamper raise paws and touch in a high five)*

Discussion Questions

1. Who cleaned up Scout's yard?
2. How did Scout and Scamper help to clean the classroom?
3. What are some things God did for His people?
4. What was the promise the people made to God?
5. What can you do to serve God?
6. How do you help at home?

God Helps Us Obey Him

Based on: Judges 6, 7—Gideon Leads God's Army
Props: none

SCAMPER: *(hugs Scout)* You are my best friend!

SCOUT: *(hugs Scamper)* You are my forever friend!

SCAMPER: We have fun together!

SCOUT: We help each other!

SCAMPER: You helped me to see into the tent!

SCOUT: *(giggles)* When you stood on my back, you were tall enough to see.

SCAMPER: I was small enough to put my head in the flap.

SCOUT: How many people were in the tent?

SCAMPER: I saw three. I saw a father, a mother, and a child.

SCOUT: What were they doing?

SCAMPER: Sleeping.

SCOUT: I guess they were camping.

SCAMPER: I think so.

SCOUT: I saw a cooler. My people put food in coolers.

SCAMPER: Will they eat at the park?

SCOUT: We did when my people took me camping.

SCAMPER: That must have been fun.

SCOUT: It was. They cooked dinner on a fire.

SCAMPER: What did they cook?

SCOUT: They roasted hot dogs.

SCAMPER: *(shocked, emphasizes)* You're a dog!

SCOUT: *(giggles)* Hot dogs are not *(emphasizes)* real dogs. They are meat.

SCAMPER: *(giggles)* What a funny name for meat!

SCOUT: I like hot dogs. I ate two!

SCAMPER: Where did you sleep?

SCOUT: I slept in the tent with the people.

SCAMPER: It sounds like fun.

SCOUT: It was! The next day, we hiked in the woods.

SCAMPER: I play in the woods every day.

SCOUT: My people obey all the rules.

SCAMPER: There are rules for camping?

SCOUT: Of course there are.

SCAMPER: What kind of rules?

SCOUT: They have to put scraps in a trash can.

SCAMPER: That's so the woods won't get smelly and junky.

SCOUT: They have to put water on the fire.

SCAMPER: Obeying the rules keeps us clean and safe.

SCOUT: God has rules too.

SCAMPER: God helps us obey Him.

Discussion Questions

1. Where did the campers sleep?
2. How did they cook?
3. Who helped Gideon obey God?
4. What instrument did Gideon blow?
5. Who teaches you to obey God?
6. Who can you help?

God Helps Us Make Good Choices

Based on: Ruth 1, 2—Ruth Makes Good Choices
Props: none

SCOUT: Hi, Scamper.

SCAMPER: Hi. *(modestly)* I helped someone today.

SCOUT: Who?

SCAMPER: A cow.

SCOUT: What happened?

SCAMPER: It kept saying *Mooo! Mooo!* I think it was crying.

SCOUT: Why would a cow cry?

SCAMPER: Its head was stuck through a fence and it couldn't get loose.

SCOUT: *(sympathetic)* Poor cow.

SCAMPER: I wanted to help.

SCOUT: *(skeptical)* You are too small to help a big cow.

SCAMPER: *(emphatically)* I *did* help the cow, Scout!

SCOUT: *(giggles)* That is funny. What did you do?

SCAMPER: I looked for a person. I knew that a person would know what to do.

SCOUT: How did you plan to tell a person when you found one? People don't understand squirrel language.

SCAMPER: That *(emphasizes) was* a big problem. I got an idea when a car went by.

SCOUT: What kind of idea?

SCAMPER: When I heard another car coming, I began to run along the fence.

SCOUT: How did that help?

SCAMPER: The people in the car watched me.

SCOUT: So?

SCAMPER: I ran to where the cow was stuck!

SCOUT: Did the people see the cow?

SCAMPER: Yep.

SCOUT: Did they help?

SCAMPER: A man and a child got out of the car.

SCOUT: What did they do?

SCAMPER: The man got the cow loose and they petted it.

SCOUT: That must have made the cow feel better.

SCAMPER: I think so. It looked happy.

SCOUT: The people didn't have to help.

SCAMPER: No, they could have kept going.

SCOUT: I'm glad they chose to help the cow.

SCOUT: God helps us make good choices.

SCAMPER: Yep. He does.

SCOUT: Let's go play!

SCAMPER: I'll race you to the tree!

Discussion Questions

1. What animal did Scamper help?
2. How did Scamper help the cow?
3. Why did Ruth stay with Naomi?
4. What food did Ruth put in her basket?
5. Who has helped you?
6. How can you help someone?

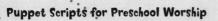

Puppet Scripts for Preschool Worship

God Uses People to Care for Us

Based on: 1 Samuel 1–3—Samuel as a Boy
Props: Place a small dog collar or ribbon around Scout's neck.

SCAMPER: *(looks at Scout)* You are dressed up today!

SCOUT: *(turns around and back)* Do you like it?

SCAMPER: You look very nice!

SCOUT: My people bought it for me.

SCAMPER: You're a lucky dog!

SCOUT: Yep!

SCAMPER: They care for you.

SCOUT: I know.

SCAMPER: You live in their comfortable house.

SCOUT: I have my own soft bed.

SCAMPER: *(surprised)* Wow! What else do you have?

SCOUT: I have bowls for food and water.

SCAMPER: *(sadly)* I don't even have one bowl.

SCOUT: I have toys. There is a ball and . . .

SCAMPER: *(interrupts)* I don't have any of those things! No one cares about me.

SCOUT: *(pats Scamper)* I care, Scamper. Don't be sad.

SCAMPER: Thanks, Scout.

SCOUT: I remember someone who cares—the person who gives you corn!

SCAMPER: *(encouraged)* There is always corn in my feeder!

SCOUT: God uses people to care for us.

SCAMPER: *(giggles)* I'm not sad anymore. I have things too.

SCOUT: You have a feeder instead of a bowl!

SCAMPER: The birds and I have water in a birdbath.

SCOUT: The person keeps it full for you.

SCAMPER: *(contentedly)* I am cared for!

Discussion Questions

1. What new thing does Scout have?
2. Who cares for Scamper?
3. Where did Samuel live?
4. Who brought a new coat to Samuel every year?
5. Who takes care of you?
6. How can you care for others?

God Wants Us to Be His Helpers

Based on: 1 Samuel 3, 8–10, 12—Samuel Serves God All His Life
Props: none

SCAMPER: What kind of dog are you, Scout?

SCOUT: I'm a sheepdog.

SCAMPER: You can't fool me! Sheepdogs are *(emphasizes)* very big!

SCOUT: I'm not fooling. I'm a small puppy now, but when I grow up, I'll be *(emphasizes)* big.

SCAMPER: Oh. You'll be *(emphasizes)* big, and I'll still be *(softly)* small.

SCOUT: That's OK, Scamper. We'll still be friends.

SCAMPER: *(surprised)* A *(emphasizes)* big dog would be friends with a *small* squirrel?

SCOUT: *(pats Scamper)* Of course! We are forever pals!

SCAMPER: I'm afraid of most *(emphasizes)* big animals.

SCOUT: Sheepdogs are gentle, Scamper.

SCAMPER: I didn't know that.

SCOUT: Oh yes, sheepdogs care for the sheep.

SCAMPER: How do they do that?

SCOUT: They chase away animals that might hurt the sheep.

SCAMPER: That would make the sheep feel safe.

SCOUT: Sheepdogs obey their farmers.

SCAMPER: What do sheepdogs do?

SCOUT: The sheep need green grass to eat and water to drink. The sheepdog guides the sheep to grass and water.

SCAMPER: How does the sheepdog know where to go?

SCOUT: The farmer tells the dog which way to go.

SCAMPER: Oh, I see. The sheepdog is the farmer's helper.

SCOUT: That's right.

SCAMPER: Does your family have sheep?

SCOUT: They don't have sheep, but I can still be a protector.

SCAMPER: How will you do that?

SCOUT: When I am *(emphasizes)* big, I won't let anything hurt my people!

SCAMPER: You will be your family's helper.

SCOUT: I will, Scamper.

SCAMPER: God wants us to be His helpers.

SCOUT: I will always obey and help!

SCAMPER: *(pats Scout)* Good boy, Scout!

Discussion Questions

1. What kind of dog is Scout?
2. What is a young dog called?
3. How was Samuel God's helper?
4. Who told Samuel what to say to the people?
5. Who is a helper in your church?
6. How can you be a helper for God?

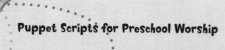

God Wants Us to Help Others

Based on: 1 Samuel 16—David Plays for Saul
Props: Place a toy keyboard next to Scamper. (Another instrument may be substituted.)

SCAMPER: *(rubs paws together, then plays the keyboard notes randomly and loudly)* I love to make music!

SCOUT: *(giggles)* Scamper, that is not music.

SCAMPER: *(irritated)* It is too music, Scout!

SCOUT: Sorry. I didn't mean to hurt your feelings.

SCAMPER: That's OK. I guess I'm not very good at this.

SCOUT: You will be if you keep practicing.

SCAMPER: Do you think so?

SCOUT: Sure you will. You can do it!

SCAMPER: *(encouraged)* OK, here goes. I'm learning to play "Silent Night." *(plays the keyboard randomly, loudly, and continuously during Scout's next line)*

SCOUT: *(holds ears and howls)* Howwwl! Howwl! Howwl!

SCAMPER: *(looks at Scout)* I told you I was playing "Silent Night." What were you singing?

SCOUT: Um . . . I guess it was "Silent Night."

SCAMPER: Try again, Scout. Follow the music this time. *(turns back to keyboard and rubs paws together)*

SCOUT: *(to himself)* I guess that means I can't cover my ears.

SCAMPER: What did you say, Scout?

SCOUT: Oh, nothing.

SCAMPER: OK, let's hear you sing while I play. *(begins to play randomly and loudly)*

SCOUT: *(sings the first words of "Silent Night" and then places paws on ears and howls)* Howwwl! Howwwl!

SCAMPER: *(sternly)* Scout, now stop that! Sing right.

SCOUT: I can't help it, Scamper. The music is so loud it hurts my ears.

SCAMPER: Oh. I'm sorry. *(pauses)* I'll play more quietly. *(turn down volume)*

SCOUT: OK, and I'll try to sing right.

SCAMPER: *(plays keyboard randomly, but softly)*

SCOUT: *(sings the first line of "Silent Night," not necessarily on key)*

SCAMPER: That was good, Scout. You helped me with my song!

SCOUT: Playing softly helped me to sing.

SCAMPER: God wants us to help others.

SCOUT: We make good music. *(giggles)*

Discussion Questions

1. What instrument did Scamper try to play?
2. How did Scout sing at first?
3. How did David help the king?
4. What instrument did David play?
5. Have you ever tried to play an instrument?
6. How can you help someone?

God Helps Us to Be Brave

Based on: 1 Samuel 17—David Meets Goliath

Props: With a wide-tip marker, draw six sheep on a sheet of paper. Use ovals for bodies and heads, straight lines for legs and ears, and dots for eyes. Hang it nearby.

SCAMPER: Look, Scout! *(points to picture)* See the sheep?

SCOUT: Lots of sheep!

SCAMPER: I wonder who drew it.

SCOUT: The girl in my family drew it.

SCAMPER: She's a good artist!

SCOUT: You're right, Scamper!

SCAMPER: How many sheep are there?

SCOUT: I don't know.

SCAMPER: Count them, Scout!

SCOUT: Um, *(pauses)* one, two, three, *(pauses)* four, um . . . *(pauses)*

SCAMPER: Come on, Scout! What comes after four?

SCOUT: *(uncertain)* Ten?

SCAMPER: No. It is five.

SCOUT: One, two, three, four, *(pauses)* um, what did you say comes next?

SCAMPER: Five, then six. One, two, three, four, five, six. Six sheep.

SCOUT: You are smart, Scamper. *(discouraged)* I wish I could count as well as you.

SCAMPER: You are learning. Soon you'll catch up to me on counting.

SCOUT: Do you think so?

SCAMPER: Of course you will.

SCOUT: I think the girl should draw a sheepdog too.

SCAMPER: To care for the sheep?

SCOUT: Yes, she should draw a brave sheepdog!

SCAMPER: Why does the sheepdog have to be brave?

SCOUT: Because sometimes bears and lions try to hurt the sheep.

SCAMPER: I'd be afraid of a bear or a lion.

SCOUT: I would be brave. Sheepdogs must be brave to protect the sheep.

SCAMPER: I am good at counting, but you are brave.

SCOUT: *(brightens)* That's true, Scamper!

SCAMPER: What makes you brave?

SCOUT: God helps us be brave.

SCAMPER: What did you do that was brave?

SCOUT: *(proudly)* I kept a mean cat from coming into our yard.

SCAMPER: That is brave. Cats can scratch!

SCOUT: *(giggles)* I kept the mean cat away!

SCAMPER: *(pats Scout)* Brave Scout!

Discussion Questions

1. Who can count to six?
2. Who is the braver?
3. What was David's job?
4. Who helped David to be brave?
5. When have you been brave?
6. How can we ask God to help us?

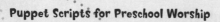

God Wants Us to Be Good Friends

Based on: 1 Samuel 18, 20—David and Jonathan
Props: Print the word *FRIEND* in large letters on a poster board and place the poster near Scout and Scamper.

Scout: Scamper, let's play!

Scamper: OK, Scout.

Scout: What shall we play today?

Scamper: Let's play a word game.

Scout: I don't know any word games.

Scamper: I do. I thought it up myself.

Scout: OK, tell me what to do.

Scamper: We are friends, right?

Scout: We are forever friends!

Scamper: Let's think of words that tell what a friend is.

Scout: OK.

Scamper: The first letter is *F. (points to* F *on poster board)* Think of a friend word that starts with the letter *F.*

Scout: *(ponders)* Hm. How about *fun*?

Scamper: That's a good one, Scout! We are friends. We have fun together.

Scout: Yep.

Scamper: OK, the next letter is *(points to* R*)* R.

Scout: That's a hard one.

Scamper: *(thinks)* It is hard. *(pauses)* Oh, I've got it! *Respect.*

Scout: That means we treat each other nicely. Good word.

Scamper: The next letter is *(points to* I*)* I.

Scout: How about *I*? *(emphasizes)* I am your friend.

Scamper: And *(emphasizes)* I am yours.

Scout: Give me another letter, Scamper!

Scamper: *(points to* E*)* E. Enjoy! We enjoy playing together.

Scout: Let me do one now, Scamper.

Scamper: *(points to* N*)* N. *(looks at Scout)*

Scout: *N.* Um. Let me think. *(pauses) Nice!*

Scamper: Very good, Scout! *(points to* D*)* D is the last one.

Scout: I can't think of one.

Scamper: How about *defend*?

Scout: That means we look after each other.

Scamper: We do that for sure.

Scout: God wants us to be good friends.

Scamper: That is what the word spells—*friend.*

Scout: We are forever friends!

Discussion Questions

1. What kind of game did Scamper and Scout play?
2. What does the word on the poster spell?
3. Who was David's friend?
4. What did David and Jonathan promise one another?
5. What is your best friend's name?
6. What fun thing do you and your friend do together?

God Wants Us to Be Kind

Based on: 2 Samuel 9—David and Mephibosheth
Props: none

SCAMPER: *(waving to Scout)* Hi, Scout. Let's play!

SCOUT: *(tilts head up with each huff and tilts head down with each puff)* Huff, puff, huff, puff. Hi, Scamper. *Huff, puff.*

SCAMPER: *(looking at Scout)* You sure are panting!

SCOUT: *(tilts head up and down as before)* Huff, puff. I was chasing a cat away! *Huff, puff.*

SCAMPER: *(catches breath while briefly placing hands over mouth)* Uh-oh. God wants us to be kind to *(emphasizing last word)* everyone.

SCOUT: *(indignantly)* I am kind!

SCAMPER: I guess that cat doesn't think you are very kind.

SCOUT: *(raising both paws)* I didn't hurt him. I was helping someone.

SCAMPER: *(tilting head toward Scout)* It is kind to help someone. Who were you helping?

SCOUT: A little squirrel. She had a hurt foot.

SCAMPER: *(looking at front paw)* I hurt my foot once. It was hard to run and climb trees.

SCOUT: *(spreads front feet and raises head distinctly at the word* pounce*)* The cat was about to pounce on that poor little squirrel!

SCAMPER: *(excitedly)* Oh no! *(knowingly)* Cats don't like us squirrels.

SCOUT: *(nodding head)* I know. The little squirrel could not get away. She needed help.

SCAMPER: *(excitedly)* She sure did!

SCOUT: *(gruffly)* I growled, *grrrrr,* and I chased the cat away! That is how I helped!

SCAMPER: *(tilting head)* What did the squirrel do?

SCOUT: *(moving front feet one at a time as though climbing slowly)* She climbed the tree with her three good feet. Soon she was safe on a high limb.

SCAMPER: Good boy! *(patting Scout)* You were kind to the little squirrel. God wants us to be kind.

Discussion Questions

1. How was Scout kind to the little squirrel?
2. How do you think the squirrel felt when Scout was kind to her?
3. How was King David kind to Mephibosheth?
4. How do you think Mephibosheth felt when King David was kind to him?
5. What kind thing can you do for someone?
6. How does God feel when we are kind?

We Can Sing to God

Based on: 2 Samuel 22; Psalms 4, 5, 23, 100, 122, 150—David Sings to God
Props: Ask someone to clap and tap his or her feet at the appropriate times for sound effects.

SCAMPER: *(singing)* If you're happy and you know it, clap your paws! *(claps twice)*

SCOUT: Can I sing too?

SCAMPER: Sure. I'll sing one line and you sing the next.

SCOUT: This will be fun! I love to sing.

SCAMPER: You're not going to howl, are you?

SCOUT: No. I'll sing nicely.

SCAMPER: OK, here goes. *(sings)* If you're happy and you know it, clap your paws. *(claps twice)*

SCOUT: *(sings)* If you're happy and you know it, clap your paws. *(claps twice)*

SCAMPER: *(sings)* If you're happy and you know it, *(places paws at side of face)* then your face will surely show it.

SCOUT: *(sings)* If you're happy and you know it, clap your paws. *(claps twice)*

SCAMPER: *(looks at children)* Hey, kids, sing with us!

SCOUT: *(sings)* If you're happy and you know it, stomp your feet. *(tilts onto one foot, then the other)*

SCAMPER: *(sings)* If you're happy and you know it, stomp your feet. *(tilts onto one foot, then the other)*

SCOUT: *(sings)* If you're happy and you know it, *(places paws at side of face)* then your face will surely show it.

SCAMPER: *(sings)* If you're happy and you know it, stomp your feet. *(tilts onto one foot, then the other)*

SCOUT: That was fun! I like to sing.

SCAMPER: Me too. God likes to hear us sing.

SCOUT: We can sing to God.

SCAMPER: Come on, Scout! Let's go think of another song to sing!

Discussion Questions

1. What did Scout and Scamper do with their paws?
2. What showed that they were happy?
3. How did David show he loved God?
4. Where can we read the songs that David wrote?
5. When do you sing?
6. What happy song can you sing?

We Can Ask God to Know Right from Wrong

Based on: 1 Kings 3, 4—Solomon Prays to Know What Is Right
Props: none

SCOUT:	Let's play follow the leader!
SCAMPER:	OK. That will be fun!
SCOUT:	You can be the leader. I will follow you.
SCAMPER:	OK. First, I'll run up the tallest tree!
SCOUT:	*(disappointed)* I can't climb trees, Scamper.
SCAMPER:	Oh yeah. I remember. I won't climb trees.
SCOUT:	Thank you.
SCAMPER:	I'll run under the fence!
SCOUT:	I'm not allowed to leave the yard!
SCAMPER:	We can run into the house through your puppy door!
SCOUT:	No, Scamper. I can't bring friends into the house.
SCAMPER:	Hm . . . I'll have to think of something else. I will run around the house.
SCOUT:	I can do that! You are a good leader, Scamper.
SCAMPER:	I'll jump over that puddle!
SCOUT:	I can jump high!
SCAMPER:	I might climb the front steps.
SCOUT:	I'll be right behind you.
SCAMPER:	We can leap from the top step to the ground.
SCOUT:	I may tumble onto the ground, but I'll follow.
SCAMPER:	You are a good follower, Scout.
SCOUT:	I'm glad we can play and not break any rules.
SCAMPER:	Your family expects you to obey the rules.
SCOUT:	Children must do right, also.
SCAMPER:	How can we know what is right, Scout?
SCOUT:	We can ask God to know right from wrong.
SCAMPER:	God watches over children and helps them.
SCOUT:	When they play follow the leader?
SCAMPER:	God helps children when they play and at other times too.
SCOUT:	When they don't know what to do?
SCAMPER:	That's right, Scout.
SCOUT:	Hey, I thought we were going to play.
SCAMPER:	We are! *(turns to walk away)* Follow me!

(Scout and Scamper walk away)

Discussion Questions

1. What game did Scout and Scamper play?
2. How was Scamper a good leader?
3. Who told King Solomon he could have one wish?
4. What did he wish for?
5. What are some rules you must obey?
6. How can you know right from wrong?

We Can Worship God Anywhere

Based on: 1 Kings 5–8—Solomon Builds the Temple
Props Place a stack of building blocks near Scout and Scamper.

SCAMPER: Hi, Scout! I see you have some blocks.

SCOUT: They belong to my family's little girl.

SCAMPER: Can we play with them?

SCOUT: *(nods)* Sure. It's OK.

SCAMPER: What shall we build?

SCOUT: Maybe a house?

SCAMPER: We can make a playhouse for you and me.

SCOUT: We could play in it when it rains.

SCAMPER: It would keep us dry.

SCOUT: What else could we make?

SCAMPER: We can build a wall.

SCOUT: We want a gate so we can walk in and out.

SCAMPER: We could invite our friends inside.

SCOUT: We could have an animal party!

SCAMPER: How about making a school?

SCOUT: You can be the teacher!

SCAMPER: I would mark your papers with good grades.

SCOUT: What if we build steps up real high?

SCAMPER: That would be fun. We could look down at all the people!

SCOUT: What if we fall down? That would hurt.

SCAMPER: I guess we won't build the steps.

SCOUT: We could make a pet food store and fill it with Puppy Crunch and corn.

SCAMPER: Yum, yum. That's the best idea yet. I love corn!

SCOUT: We have to find some bowls to put the food in.

SCAMPER: I don't have a bowl.

SCOUT: I have one, but it has to stay in the house.

SCAMPER: What else can we build with the blocks?

SCOUT: Let's make a church building!

SCAMPER: It will have a steeple on top pointing to Heaven!

SCOUT: We will invite the children to come inside.

SCAMPER: *(giggles)* There are not enough blocks for them to get inside.

SCOUT: *(looks at blocks)* You're right. Oh well, it was fun to think about.

SCAMPER: The children can worship God here in class.

SCOUT: We can all worship God anywhere.

Discussion Questions

1. What did Scout and Scamper have to play with?
2. What is one thing they thought of building?
3. What did Solomon build?
4. How did Solomon thank God?
5. What can you build with blocks?
6. How can you worship God?

God Provides for Us

Based on: 1 Kings 17—Elijah Is Fed by Ravens
Props: Set a bottle of water nearby.

SCAMPER: *(looks at bottle of water)* That's a lot of water!

SCOUT: You can have a drink.

SCAMPER: I can't pick up that big bottle!

SCOUT: I guess not. *(pauses)* Hey, where does water come from, anyway?

SCAMPER: *(points paw at bottle)* This water comes from a bottle. *(giggles)*

SCOUT: Silly Scamper. Where did they get it to put it into the bottle?

SCAMPER: I think it comes from natural springs.

SCOUT: The springs I saw had leaves in them. Frogs too!

SCAMPER: *(looks at bottle)* Yuk! I don't want to drink frog water!

SCOUT: *(looks at label)* It doesn't say anything about frogs *(pauses)* or leaves.

SCAMPER: *(looks at label)* Wow! Look at that *(emphasizes)* big word!

SCOUT: *(pauses between syllables)* Purr . . . i . . . *(excited)* fried! Purrifried!

SCAMPER: Fried water? I don't think they can do that.

SCOUT: You figure it out.

SCAMPER: *(pauses between syllables)* Pur . . . i . . . fied. Purified. That means it is pure.

SCOUT: Pure?

SCAMPER: Yeah, that means there is no dirt, leaves, *(pauses)* or frogs in it.

SCOUT: *(giggles)* It must be good to drink.

SCAMPER: I've seen lots of people drinking from bottles like that.

SCOUT: *(excited)* I know where else water comes from!

SCAMPER: Where?

SCOUT: Rain! Rain falls from the sky and fills up the streams!

SCAMPER: I listen while rain drips softly on my tree.

SCOUT: I like to hear it on my doghouse roof when I fall asleep.

SCAMPER: God sends the rain.

SCOUT: God provides water for us.

SCAMPER: Water is good.

SCOUT: It is good to drink.

SCAMPER: Playing in the rain is fun too!

SCOUT: I like to splash in puddles.

SCAMPER: Rain washes the whole world clean!

SCOUT: I like the fresh smell after a rain!

SCAMPER: Hurry, Scout! I see a cloud outside the window. Maybe rain is coming!

Discussion Questions

1. What do Scout and Scamper like to drink?
2. What water falls from the sky?
3. Where did Elijah get water?
4. Who brought food to Elijah?
5. How do you get clean?
6. What good drink can be made with water?

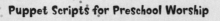

We Can Obey God by Sharing

Based on: 1 Kings 17—Elijah Helps a Widow

Props: Place one-fourth of a peanut butter and jelly sandwich between Scout and Scamper. To avoid soiling the puppets, leave it out overnight to dry.

SCOUT: Hey, Scamper. My girl gave me a sandwich. Do you want to share?

SCAMPER: *(looks at sandwich, hesitantly)* I don't know. Is it dog food?

SCOUT: No. It is bread.

SCAMPER: *(curious)* What's in it?

SCOUT: Peanut butter.

SCAMPER: *(sniffs sandwich)* Sniff. It smells like nuts!

SCOUT: That's what it is, Scamper. It is made of peanuts.

SCAMPER: *(looks at sandwich)* Is it crunchy?

SCOUT: No. The nuts are all squashed up.

SCAMPER: Why would anyone do that?

SCOUT: *(exasperated)* Scamper! It is squashed so it will spread on bread!

SCAMPER: Oh. What's that purple stuff?

SCOUT: It's jelly.

SCAMPER: I suppose it is squashed too.

SCOUT: This jelly is made from grapes, all cooked and stirred.

SCAMPER: People do funny things with their food, don't they?

SCOUT: *(giggles)* Maybe they do, but this is good.

SCAMPER: I like nuts. And I like grapes.

SCOUT: You'll like this, Scamper. Try it!

SCAMPER: *(carefully nibbles at sandwich)* Mmm, yummy! *(nibbles again)*

SCOUT: I told you it was good! *(nibbles at sandwich)*

SCAMPER: You were right! *(nibbles at sandwich)* This is great!

SCOUT: *(nibbles at sandwich)* I love peanut butter and jelly sandwiches!

SCAMPER: *(looks at Scout)* Thank you for sharing.

SCOUT: We are friends. We share everything!

SCAMPER: Yep.

SCOUT: The Bible says to share with others.

SCAMPER: God wants us to obey Him, and we can obey God by sharing.

SCOUT: I obeyed, didn't I?

SCAMPER: Yes. You're a good dog, Scout. *(pats Scout)*

SCOUT: *(happily)* I'm glad you liked the sandwich, Scamper.

SCAMPER: I'll share your sandwiches any time, Scout.

Discussion Questions

1. What did Scout share with Scamper?
2. Why does Scamper like peanut butter?
3. Why couldn't Elijah drink from the brook?
4. What did the widow make for Elijah?
5. What do you like to eat on your bread?
6. Can you make a peanut butter and jelly sandwich? How?

God Listens to Our Prayers

Based on: 1 Kings 17—Elijah Helps a Widow's Son
Props: none

SCAMPER: Where have you been all week, Scout?

SCOUT: I was in the house.

SCAMPER: I wanted you to play outside with me.

SCOUT: I know, but I was needed inside.

SCAMPER: Who needed you?

SCOUT: My girl was sick.

SCAMPER: What was wrong with her?

SCOUT: She had chicken pox!

SCAMPER: Did she catch it from a chicken?

SCOUT: (giggles) Silly Scamper! That's not how you get chicken pox!

SCAMPER: I'm glad to hear that!

SCOUT: Chicken pox is a childhood illness.

SCAMPER: Did she have a fever?

SCOUT: A little. Some medicine made her feel better.

SCAMPER: I'm glad she feels better.

SCOUT: She had some red spots on her skin.

SCAMPER: Was she polka-dotted?

SCOUT: (nods) Uh-huh, she was.

SCAMPER: It's no fun to be sick.

SCOUT: She was sad because she had to stay indoors.

SCAMPER: So you stayed in to play with her?

SCOUT: Yes.

SCAMPER: What did you play with her?

SCOUT: I did all my tricks and made her smile.

SCAMPER: What else?

SCOUT: I chased my tail to make her laugh.

SCAMPER: (giggles) You are funny when you do that!

SCOUT: Her mother brought juice for her to drink.

SCAMPER: Juice is good.

SCOUT: She had chicken soup at lunch.

SCAMPER: Does chicken soup make you get chicken pox?

SCOUT: (giggles) No, silly Scamper! Soup is good for sick people.

SCAMPER: Her mother knew how to care for the girl.

SCOUT: The girl is better now.

SCAMPER: That's good.

SCOUT: I sat next to her as she said her bedtime prayers.

SCAMPER: God listens to our prayers.

SCOUT: She is well. Now we can play!

SCAMPER: I'll race you to the big tree!

Discussion Questions

1. Who was sick?
2. How did Scout help?
3. What happened to the widow's son?
4. What did Elijah do to help?
5. Who cares for you when you are sick?
6. Who can help you get well?

God Is Powerful

Based on: 1 Kings 18—Elijah and the Prophets of Baal
Props: none

SCAMPER: We had fun yesterday!

SCOUT: We sure did! I love the zoo!

SCAMPER: The ostrich is a funny bird!

SCOUT: It is strong.

SCAMPER: Those legs ran fast!

SCOUT: What about the gorilla?

SCAMPER: It's strong too.

SCOUT: It has *(emphasizes) big* muscles.

SCAMPER: I'm not afraid of it!

SCOUT: You would be if it got out of the cage!

SCAMPER: I would run fast!

SCOUT: So would I.

SCAMPER: A lion is stronger than a gorilla!

SCOUT: Did you see the lion's teeth and claws?

SCAMPER: It is a powerful animal.

SCOUT: Its hair is a pretty color.

SCAMPER: I liked its tail.

SCOUT: Bears are big and hairy.

SCAMPER: The mother bear is huge!

SCOUT: She has a cute cub.

SCAMPER: If someone bothered the cub, that person would be in trouble!

SCOUT: Oh, man! I'll stay away from any bear cubs I see.

SCAMPER: What animal do you think is the strongest?

SCOUT: The elephant!

SCAMPER: I think so too.

SCOUT: Did you see the size of its feet?

SCAMPER: *(looks at paws)* Its feet were bigger than mine.

SCOUT: *(looks at Scampers paws)* Yep. Lots bigger!

SCAMPER: It has a powerful trunk!

SCOUT: Did you see the elephant pick up that log with its trunk?

SCAMPER: That was awesome!

SCOUT: It likes to eat peanuts.

SCAMPER: I know. I gave it some of mine.

SCOUT: The elephant is the winner! It is the strongest!

SCAMPER: I know who is stronger than an elephant.

SCOUT: No way!

SCAMPER: Yes! I'm not talking about an animal.

SCOUT: *(understanding)* Oh. You mean God?

SCAMPER: God is powerful.

SCOUT: He is stronger than any person or animal.

SCAMPER: He is awesome!

Discussion Questions

1. What was the strongest animal at the zoo?
2. What did the elephant lift?
3. Who told the people about God?
4. Who made the wood burn?
5. How powerful is God?
6. What can God do that people cannot do?

We Can Please God by Helping Others

Based on: 2 Kings 4—Elisha and a Widow's Oil
Props: Place a small, empty cup with a straw in it near Scout and Scamper.

SCOUT: *(drinks from the straw)* Mmm, this is good!

SCAMPER: I'm thirsty. May I have some?

SCOUT: Sure, Scamper. *(pushes cup toward Scamper)*

SCAMPER: *(drinks from straw)* Thank you for sharing.

SCOUT: You're welcome.

SCAMPER: This is a big drink.

SCOUT: It is almost as big as you and me!

SCAMPER: I think all the animals in the forest could have a drink.

SCOUT: Probably. I wonder if it would be enough?

SCAMPER: Maybe. There is a lot there.

SCOUT: I want some more. *(drinks from straw)*

SCAMPER: Me too. *(drinks from straw)*

SCOUT: Man! This is never going to run out!

SCAMPER: *(giggles)* It would be nice to have an unending drink.

SCOUT: We'd never be thirsty again!

SCAMPER: Nope! Never again.

SCOUT: *(drinks from straw)* I'm getting full.

SCAMPER: *(drinks from straw)* Me too, Scout.

SCOUT: I'm glad I could share with you.

SCAMPER: You are a good dog, Scout. *(pats Scout)*

SCOUT: You were thirsty.

SCAMPER: You helped me by giving me a drink.

SCOUT: We can help others.

SCAMPER: Helping others pleases God.

SCOUT: I think I'll have just one more sip. *(drinks from straw)*

SCAMPER: I'll have some more too. *(drinks from straw)*

SCOUT: *(looks into cup)* There is some left. *(drinks from straw)*

SCAMPER: My turn! *(drinks from straw and makes sound of air being sucked into straw)*

SCOUT: Uh-oh. I think it is gone, Scamper.

SCAMPER: *(looks into cup, surprised)* It is all gone.

SCOUT: Let me try. *(makes sound of sucking air into straw, looks into cup)* There is no more.

SCAMPER: It lasted until we weren't thirsty anymore.

SCOUT: Uh-huh, it did. I'm glad we had enough.

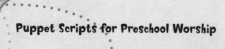

Discussion Questions

1. How did Scout help Scamper?
2. What sound did you hear when the drink was gone?
3. Who helped the widow?
4. What happened to the empty containers?
5. Who can you help?
6. How can you help that person?

God Wants Us to Share with Others

Based on: 2 Kings 4—Elisha and a Shunammite Family
Props: none

SCOUT: Hi, Scamper.

SCAMPER: Hello, Scout. What's up?

SCOUT: I get to sleep overnight in my new doghouse.

SCAMPER: I thought you always slept in the house in a doggie bed.

SCOUT: I do, but it is warm outside and my family said I could stay out.

SCAMPER: Cool. I saw the doghouse. It is nice.

SCOUT: Why don't you stay with me tonight?

SCAMPER: You mean, like a sleepover?

SCOUT: Sure. It will be fun!

SCAMPER: I've never been on a sleepover before.

SCOUT: Me either. Let's do it!

SCAMPER: OK. I'll have to go ask my mom first.

SCOUT: Do you think she will let you?

SCAMPER: I think so. She just wants to know that I am safe.

SCOUT: You will be safe here.

SCAMPER: Oh boy, this will be so much fun!

SCOUT: We can talk all night if we want.

SCAMPER: We can sleep in late tomorrow.

SCOUT: I'll share my dinner with you.

SCAMPER: Puppy Crunch? I don't like dog food.

SCOUT: There is a piece of bread in my bowl too. Do you like bread?

SCAMPER: I do! Sometimes the person who fills my feeder leaves bread for me.

SCOUT: We can share the bread.

SCAMPER: God wants us to share with others.

SCOUT: We always share.

SCAMPER: Because we are best friends.

SCOUT: If other animals come along, we would share with them too.

SCAMPER: Sure we would. We would even let them stay all night with us.

SCOUT: We could have an animal slumber party!

SCAMPER: Whoopee! I'm glad you are sleeping outside tonight.

SCOUT: Me too, Scamper.

SCAMPER: I'm going to ask my mom right now!

Discussion Questions

1. Where is Scout going to sleep?
2. What will Scout and Scamper share?
3. What did the woman and her husband do for Elisha?
4. What promise did Elisha make to the woman?
5. What do you have to share?
6. Who can you share with?

Puppet Scripts for Preschool Worship

55

God Has Power to Help Us

Based on: 2 Kings 4—Elisha and the Shunammites' Son
Props: none

SCAMPER:	Hey, Scout. Let's play in my nest!
SCOUT:	Funny Scamper! I can't climb a tree!
SCAMPER:	I forgot.
SCOUT:	*(wistfully)* I'd like to visit your home.
SCAMPER:	I think if you tried, you could climb.
SCOUT:	Scamper, I tried yesterday, remember?
SCAMPER:	Oh yeah. You tried to dig your toenails into the bark.
SCOUT:	Why won't it work? *(looks at toenails)* They are sharp.
SCAMPER:	*(touches Scout's toenails with his paw)* Yep, they are.
SCOUT:	Let me see your toenails, Scamper.
SCAMPER:	*(holds out paw while Scout looks)*
SCOUT:	Wow! You have *(emphasizes)* long toenails!
SCAMPER:	*(looks at own toenails)* They are long so I can grab and hold onto the tree branches.
SCOUT:	See, mine are short. *(holds out toenails so Scamper can see)*
SCAMPER:	*(looks at Scout's toenails)* They are too short, Scout! It is impossible for you to climb a tree!
SCOUT:	*(disappointedly)* But I want to!
SCAMPER:	*(soothingly)* I know.

SCOUT:	*(sadly)* You came to my house to play. I want to play at your house.
SCAMPER:	*(sadly)* I wish I knew what to do.
SCOUT:	Me too. I guess no one can help me.
SCAMPER:	*(brightening)* Hey! I have an idea!
SCOUT:	You do?
SCAMPER:	*(excited)* Yes! A while ago a man nailed boards on the tree next to mine so he could climb up.
SCOUT:	How can that help me?
SCAMPER:	I've seen you climb a fence. You can climb the boards in the same way.
SCOUT:	*(uncertain)* It is the wrong tree, Scamper.
SCAMPER:	I know, but the branch my nest is in reaches over to the boards!
SCOUT:	Really? I think I can do that!
SCAMPER:	The man helped us.
SCOUT:	He sure did!
SCAMPER:	People have a helper too.
SCOUT:	You mean, *(pauses)* God?
SCAMPER:	God has power to help us.
SCOUT:	We'll have fun!
SCAMPER:	OK!

Discussion Questions

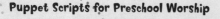

1. Where did Scout want to go?
2. Who helped Scout?
3. Who did the woman ask for help?
4. What did Elisha do for the boy?
5. Who has power to help us?
6. Who can you pray for?

God Wants Us to Worship Him

Based on: 2 Kings 5—Elisha and Naaman
Props: Place a red ribbon around Scout's neck.

SCAMPER:	*(wiping face with paws)*
SCOUT:	What are you doing, Scamper?
SCAMPER:	I'm cleaning my face.
SCOUT:	Oh.
SCAMPER:	*(continues wiping face with paws)* That should do it.
SCOUT:	*(looks at Scamper's face)* It doesn't look any different to me.
SCAMPER:	You mean it is still dirty?
SCOUT:	No. I just mean it is still the same color.
SCAMPER:	Of course it is! What did you expect?
SCOUT:	When I wash dirt off my face, it becomes white.
SCAMPER:	*(giggles)* Funny Scout! That is because your fur is white!
SCOUT:	*(giggles)* When I get dirty, it isn't.
SCAMPER:	When your face is muddy, it is almost the same color as mine.
SCOUT:	*(looks at Scamper's face)* You're right. Your fur is different from mine!
SCAMPER:	I have red fur.

SCOUT:	You do not! It is kind of reddish brown. *(places paw on ribbon)* This ribbon is red!
SCAMPER:	We are called red squirrels!
SCOUT:	Hm . . . who named your kind of squirrel? *(giggles)* Whoever it was didn't know colors.
SCAMPER:	*(giggles)* People are different colors too.
SCOUT:	Yep.
SCAMPER:	I wonder why people are different?
SCOUT:	That's how God made them.
SCAMPER:	Yep. He made lots of wonderful colors!
SCOUT:	Inside us, where we think and feel, we are just alike.
SCAMPER:	We are, Scout. *(thoughtfully)* I wonder if people are the same inside too?
SCOUT:	They must be. My girl has friends who look different on the outside.
SCAMPER:	God is pleased with everything He made.
SCOUT:	He wants all people to love each other and to love Him.
SCAMPER:	God wants us to worship Him.

Discussion Questions

1. How are Scout and Scamper the same?
2. How are Scout and Scamper different?
3. How was Naaman different from other people?
4. What happened after Naaman washed in the river?
5. How are you the same as, or different from, your friends?
6. How can we worship God?

We Can Read God's Word

Based on: 2 Kings 22, 23—Josiah Reads God's Word
Props: none

SCOUT: What were you doing all morning, Scamper?

SCAMPER: I was cleaning my squirrel nest.

SCOUT: Why?

SCAMPER: It was a big mess!

SCOUT: Oh. *(pauses)* How messy could a squirrel nest be?

SCAMPER: It can be really messy! There were cobwebs!

SCOUT: No one wants cobwebs in their home.

SCAMPER: I like to eat my acorns in the nest.

SCOUT: Acorns don't have crumbs, do they?

SCAMPER: Not crumbs, but there were lots of nut shells.

SCOUT: That sounds like a big job.

SCAMPER: It was, but I cleaned it up!

SCOUT: You even got some nut shells in your fur. *(brushes Scamper's fur with paw)* I'll brush them off.

SCAMPER: *(looks at fur)* Thank you, Scout. Am I clean now?

SCOUT: You look fine.

SCAMPER: I seem to get dirty when I clean the nest.

SCOUT: It's no wonder, with all the stuff you collect.

SCAMPER: Don't you have to clean your house?

SCOUT: No. The mother does that.

SCAMPER: What if you make a mess?

SCOUT: I get into trouble if I make a mess, then the mother cleans it up.

SCAMPER: What kind of mess do you make?

SCOUT: Sometimes my feet are muddy.

SCAMPER: Dirty tracks, huh?

SCOUT: Yes. I'm supposed to wait until someone wipes my feet when I come inside.

SCAMPER: It is good to keep things clean and fixed up.

SCOUT: The mother dusts *(emphasizes)* everything!

SCAMPER: Really?

SCOUT: She even dusts the Bible!

SCAMPER: That's good. It will be ready when someone wants to read it.

SCOUT: My people like to read it every day.

SCAMPER: We can read God's Word.

SCOUT: *(giggles)* Or we can listen, if we can't read.

SCAMPER: We can listen to God's Word too.

Discussion Questions

1. How is Scamper helping at his home?
2. What did Scout brush off of Scamper's fur?
3. What book did the priests read to Josiah?
4. What did Josiah do after hearing the Word of God?
5. How can you help keep your classroom clean?
6. What is another way you can know what the Bible says if you can't read?

Puppet Scripts for Preschool Worship

We Can Ask God for His Help

Based on: 2 Chronicles 17, 20—Jehoshaphat Asks for God's Help

Props: Hang a small round cardboard tag on a collar or ribbon that is fastened to Scout's neck.

SCAMPER: Where were you? I've looked everywhere!

SCOUT: I just got home. I was lost!

SCAMPER: Lost? How did that happen?

SCOUT: I was playing at the park with the little girl.

SCAMPER: The park is fun.

SCOUT: It is fun as long as you are not lost.

SCAMPER: Why didn't you stay with the girl?

SCOUT: She was swinging, so I laid down under a tree for a nap.

SCAMPER: Uh-oh. You weren't paying attention.

SCOUT: When I awoke, she was gone!

SCAMPER: Did you look for her?

SCOUT: I smelled the trail and tried to follow her.

SCAMPER: Did you find her?

SCOUT: No. The trail stopped at the parking lot.

SCAMPER: She must've gotten into the family car.

SCOUT: That's what happened. *(sadly)* They forgot me.

SCAMPER: Poor Scout. *(pats Scout)* Were you afraid?

SCOUT: I sure was!

SCAMPER: What did you do?

SCOUT: I barked and barked until someone came.

SCAMPER: Did the person know what to do?

SCOUT: Yes, he looked at my tag and called my people.

SCAMPER: Your family must have been happy that you were found.

SCOUT: They were, and so was I! I was scared all alone.

SCAMPER: Sometimes children are afraid too.

SCOUT: When they are lost?

SCAMPER: Yes, and at other times.

SCOUT: I'm afraid of storms.

SCAMPER: I'm afraid of cats.

SCOUT: I know how it feels to need help. Does someone help the kids?

SCAMPER: God does. We can ask God for His help.

SCOUT: I'm glad God is always listening.

Discussion Questions

1. Who was lost?
2. Who helped Scout?
3. Who did Jehoshaphat ask for help?
4. How did Jehoshaphat show his love for God?
5. What makes you afraid?
6. Who helps you when you are afraid?

God Helps Us All the Time

Based on: Nehemiah 1, 2, 4, 6—Nehemiah Rebuilds the Wall
Props: Place a broken bowl near Scout.

SCAMPER: *(looks at bowl)* What happened, Scout?

SCOUT: My bowl got broken.

SCAMPER: How?

SCOUT: I was playing with my girl. She set it on top of the doghouse.

SCAMPER: Did it fall?

SCOUT: *(sadly)* I sort of made it fall. I was jumping, barking, and wagging.

SCAMPER: You were on the doghouse roof?

SCOUT: It is fun!

SCAMPER: Did you break the bowl on purpose?

SCOUT: No. It fell when I jumped onto the roof.

SCAMPER: Uh-oh.

SCOUT: I can't fix it!

SCAMPER: Now where will they put your Puppy Crunch?

SCOUT: My owner can fix it.

SCAMPER: Are you sure?

SCOUT: Yep. He knows how to fix broken things. It's his job.

SCAMPER: He fixes broken things?

SCOUT: Last week he fixed a lady's crooked door.

SCAMPER: What else can he fix?

SCOUT: He built a whole wall that a storm had damaged.

SCAMPER: That's a *(emphasizes)* big job!

SCOUT: Our fence was falling down. He built it up again.

SCAMPER: He must be strong.

SCOUT: He used boards and nails to fix the wobbly tree house.

SCAMPER: That will keep the children safe.

SCOUT: He fixes their toys too.

SCAMPER: That must make the kids happy.

SCOUT: He likes to make people happy by helping.

SCAMPER: God makes us happy too.

SCOUT: God helps us all the time.

SCAMPER: *(pauses)* Scout, will you be in trouble?

SCOUT: No. It was an accident.

SCAMPER: You have a good owner.

SCOUT: I know.

SCAMPER: *(giggles)* You get too excited when you play!

SCOUT: *(giggles)* Yep.

Discussion Questions

1. What happened to Scout's bowl?
2. What will Scout's owner do for Scout?
3. What did Nehemiah say was broken?
4. What did Nehemiah ask the king?
5. What broken thing has someone fixed for you?
6. Who helps you by fixing broken things?

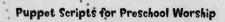

God Helps Us to Help Others

Based on: Esther 2–5, 7, 8—Esther Helps God's People
Props: Place a construction-paper crown loosely on Scamper's head.

SCOUT: Hi Scamper. *(looks at crown)* That's pretty.

SCAMPER: You can call me *(emphasizes)* King Scamper!

SCOUT: *(bows)* Yes, sir, *King* Scamper!

SCAMPER: *(bossily)* I am the king and I will tell everyone else what to do.

SCOUT: *(bows)* What shall I do, *King* Scamper?

SCAMPER: You can be my servant.

SCOUT: OK.

SCAMPER: You will obey me.

SCOUT: Yes sir!

SCAMPER: Now what can I have my servant do for me?

SCOUT: I could sing for you. *(howls)* Howl. Howl. Howl.

SCAMPER: *(tucks face and reaches paws toward ears)* Stop it, Scout!

SCOUT: You don't like my song?

SCAMPER: You can only sing if I tell you to.

SCOUT: *(bows)* Sorry, King Scamper.

SCAMPER: You can clean my castle.

SCOUT: I will play like I'm cleaning a pretend castle. *(makes motions of cleaning)* Sweep. Sweep. Dust. Polish. Scrub.

SCAMPER: Now it is time for lunch. *(points away from Scout)* Gather some nuts!

SCOUT: *(makes gathering motions)* Gather. Gather. *(motions as though laying nuts at Scamper's feet)* Here you are, King.

SCAMPER: I want real nuts!

SCOUT: *(angrily)* You are a bossy king! I quit!

SCAMPER: Don't quit, Scout! I'm sorry.

SCOUT: I don't want to be the servant anymore.

SCAMPER: I'll be a nice king.

SCOUT: You will?

SCAMPER: I'll do things to help those in my kingdom.

SCOUT: *(happily)* Like me?

SCAMPER: Yes. Ask for what you want.

SCOUT: I want to rest.

SCAMPER: I will make today a holiday. No one has to work.

SCOUT: That's more like it.

SCAMPER: I don't want to be a bossy king. *(pushes off crown and hugs Scout)* You are my *(emphasizes)* best friend!

SCOUT: *(hugs Scamper)* You could be a good king.

SCAMPER: If I were a real king, I could help others.

SCOUT: God helps us to help others.

Discussion Questions

1. Who pretended to be king?
2. Why did Scout want to quit playing?
3. Who was the new queen?
4. How did Esther help others?
5. Who do you like to pretend to be?
6. How can you help others?

We Can Obey God

Based on: Daniel 1—Daniel and His Friends Obey God
Props: none

SCAMPER:	I feel good today!
SCOUT:	*(looks at Scamper)* You *(emphasizes) look* good too!
SCAMPER:	Thank you, Scout!
SCOUT:	Your fur is shiny and soft. *(feels Scamper's fur)*
SCAMPER:	*(rubs stomach)* I am soft! *(feels Scout's fur)* You have soft, shiny fur too.
SCOUT:	*(looks at stomach and nods)* Uh-huh. That's because we are healthy.
SCAMPER:	*(curiously)* I wonder how we got so healthy?
SCOUT:	It's because we eat good food.
SCAMPER:	I eat lots of nuts, corn, and seeds.
SCOUT:	Don't forget, sometimes you eat bread from my bowl.
SCAMPER:	You are nice to share with me.
SCOUT:	I'd share all my food with you if you wanted.
SCAMPER:	Puppy Crunch? Yuk! I don't like dog food.
SCOUT:	I know. Puppy Crunch is a healthy food for dogs.
SCAMPER:	What other healthy foods do you eat?
SCOUT:	Dog biscuits and bones.
SCAMPER:	Your family feeds you very well.
SCOUT:	They care for me.
SCAMPER:	People help take care of me too.
SCOUT:	They do? I thought you gathered your own food.
SCAMPER:	I gather acorns and other nuts. Sometimes the people hang corn from my tree.
SCOUT:	Is it good for you?
SCAMPER:	Oh, yes, and it tastes yummy!
SCOUT:	It takes good food to keep us healthy and strong.
SCAMPER:	I am strong. I can run fast!
SCOUT:	I can keep up with you.
SCAMPER:	Running makes us grow stronger.
SCOUT:	I love to run. It is my favorite exercise.
SCAMPER:	I like to run up, down, and around trees!
SCOUT:	I can't do that, but I can run on the ground.
SCAMPER:	I am glad we are healthy.
SCOUT:	God wants us to take care of our bodies.
SCAMPER:	We can obey God.
SCOUT:	I'll race you to the corner!
SCAMPER:	Ready, set, go!

Discussion Questions

1. What food makes Scamper healthy?
2. What exercise does Scout like?
3. Why didn't Daniel eat the king's food?
4. Who was stronger, Daniel, or the king's men?
5. Can you name a healthy food?
6. What healthy drink do you like?

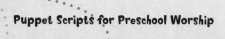

We Can Worship God

Based on: Daniel 3—Daniel's Friends Worship Only God
Props: Place a small figurine of a person (preferably a woman) nearby.

SCOUT: Good morning, Scamper.

SCAMPER: Hi, Scout. *(breathless)* I've been to the park. I ran all the way home!

SCOUT: Why?

SCAMPER: I was scared.

SCOUT: There is nothing scary at the park.

SCAMPER: Yes there is. It is a *(emphasizes)* huge woman!

SCOUT: How big?

SCAMPER: She is taller than the park gate!

SCOUT: People don't grow that big.

SCAMPER: This one did!

SCOUT: What did she do?

SCAMPER: Nothing. She just stood there.

SCOUT: Was she holding a basket?

SCAMPER: How did you know?

SCOUT: It is a statue, Scamper. You don't have to be afraid.

SCAMPER: Are you sure?

SCOUT: Statues just stand there.

SCAMPER: Why?

SCOUT: People like to look at statues.

SCAMPER: Why?

SCOUT: It is art, Scamper.

SCAMPER: Then the artist did a good job. She looked real!

SCOUT: Believe me. She won't hurt you.

SCAMPER: Can she run and play as we do?

SCOUT: Nope. She can't even move.

SCAMPER: I wonder what she is thinking.

SCOUT: *(giggles)* Statues don't have brains! They can't think.

SCAMPER: Really?

SCOUT: They are made of metal and stone. They are not alive.

SCAMPER: Oh.

SCOUT: The birds aren't afraid of her.

SCAMPER: They're not?

SCOUT: Birds sit on statues.

SCAMPER: *(giggles)* I wonder if they will build a nest in her hair?

SCOUT: They might. *(giggles)* A bird nest would make a nice hat!

SCAMPER: It would be a singing hat! *(imitates birds in high-pitched voice)* Tweet. Tweet. Tweet.

SCOUT: *(giggles)* Funny Scamper.

SCAMPER: I guess I can't talk to her.

SCOUT: Nope. She can't hear you.

SCAMPER: God hears us when we talk to Him.

SCOUT: That's right. We can worship God.

SCAMPER: I'm going back to the park. I'm not afraid now.

Discussion Questions

1. Why was Scamper afraid?
2. What can a statue do?
3. What was the king's new rule?
4. What did Daniel's friends decide not to do?
5. Who do we worship?
6. How can we worship God?

Puppet Scripts for Preschool Worship

We Can Tell About God

Based on: Daniel 5—Daniel and the Handwriting on the Wall

Props: Print the word *SCOUT* in large letters on a small piece of paper. Fasten the paper to Scout's paw with tape or an out of sight pin.

SCOUT: Look what I have, Scamper!

SCAMPER: A paper?

SCOUT: It is a special paper!

SCAMPER: Let me see. *(looks at paper)*

SCOUT: Do you know what it says?

SCAMPER: *(looks at paper)* It says "Scout"!

SCOUT: That's me.

SCAMPER: Did you write your name?

SCOUT: No. My girl did it.

SCAMPER: Is she learning to spell and write?

SCOUT: Yes. The schoolteacher is helping her learn.

SCAMPER: *(looks at paper)* She did a neat job.

SCOUT: *(looks at paper)* Uh-huh. She gave it to me.

SCAMPER: That's nice, Scout.

SCOUT: Can you write your name?

SCAMPER: Yes. Can you?

SCOUT: Not yet.

SCAMPER: I will teach you.

SCOUT: We can play a game of animal school!

SCAMPER: OK.

SCOUT: We can invite all our friends to play.

SCAMPER: I will be the teacher.

SCOUT: That will be fun!

SCAMPER: We will play after church.

SCOUT: We are learning here too, along with the children.

SCAMPER: We are all learning about God.

SCOUT: We can share what we learn with others.

SCAMPER: We can tell others about God.

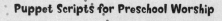

Discussion Questions

1. What did Scout's girl write?
2. What will Scamper help Scout learn to do?
3. Who wrote on the wall?
4. What did Daniel say about God?
5. Can you write your name?
6. What color would you choose to write your name?

Puppet Scripts for Preschool Worship

We Can Pray to God

Based on: Daniel 6—Daniel and the Lions' Den

Props: Find a stuffed animal that roars when pressed. Or find a stuffed toy of an animal that would make a roaring noise. You or a hidden helper can make the roaring sound each time it is called for in the script. Keep the toy out of sight but where Scamper can grasp it.

(toy roars)

Scamper: *(looks around)* What was that?

Scout: I don't know!

(toy roars)

Scamper: There it is again!

Scout: It sounds like a fierce animal.

Scamper: Maybe a bear?

Scout: Maybe a tiger!

Scamper: What is it doing here?

Scout: *(snuggles up to Scamper)* I'm scared, Scamper.

Scamper: *(puts arm around Scout and speaks bravely)* Don't worry. I'll keep you safe.

Scout: Thank you, Scamper.

(toy roars)

Scamper: I heard it again! I wonder what it is.

Scout: *(hides behind Scamper)*

Scamper: You stay here, Scout. I'll find out.

Scout: You are brave. *(hides eyes)*

Scamper: *(goes to where toy is hidden)* Here it is! *(drags toy into view and drops it between Scamper and Scout)*

Scout: *(peeking from behind paws)* What is it, Scamper?

Scamper: It is a toy animal!

Scout: It makes a lot of noise for a toy!

Scamper: I'll show you how it works. *(presses for roar)*

(toy roars)

Scout: *(jumps back)* That surprised me!

Scamper: Press right here. *(places paw on animal)* You can do it.

Scout: *(hesitates)* OK, I'll try. *(presses toy for roar)*

(toy roars)

Scamper: You did it, Scout! You are not afraid.

Scout: I am brave now.

Scamper: *(giggles)* Yes, you are brave.

Scout: I like this animal.

Scamper: I like to hear its roar.

Scout: So do I! *(presses for roar)*

(toy roars)

Scamper: *(giggles)* You are not afraid anymore.

Scout: Nope.

Scamper: When we are afraid, we can ask God to help.

Scout: God keeps us safe.

Scamper: We can pray to God.

Discussion Questions

1. Why was Scout afraid?
2. What made the noise?
3. With what furry animals did Daniel sleep?
4. Who kept Daniel safe?
5. Are you afraid of something?
6. What can you do when you are afraid?

God Wants Us to Tell About Him

Based on: Jonah 1–3—Jonah Tells About God
Props: Place a large seashell with the opening upward near Scout and Scamper.

SCAMPER: *(looks at seashell)* Hey, Scout, what is this?

SCOUT: It is a seashell.

SCAMPER: Where did you get it?

SCOUT: It came from the ocean.

SCAMPER: It did?

SCOUT: You can find seashells on the beach.

SCAMPER: Cool!

SCOUT: Put your ear against it, like this. *(places ear against seashell opening)*

SCAMPER: *(places ear against seashell opening)* Hey, I hear something!

SCOUT: It sounds like the ocean.

SCAMPER: *(places ear against seashell opening)* It has a nice sound!

SCOUT: I have fun by the water.

SCAMPER: Do you swim?

SCOUT: Mostly I splash.

SCAMPER: What do the children do?

SCOUT: They play in the sand with buckets and shovels.

SCAMPER: Are there fish?

SCOUT: Lots of fish! There are turtles too.

SCAMPER: *(giggles)* Turtles like to play peek-a-boo.

SCOUT: *(giggles)* They pull their heads inside their shells to hide. They peek out when you are not looking.

SCAMPER: Thanks for telling me about the ocean, Scout.

SCOUT: You're welcome. I like to tell happy things.

SCAMPER: We tell about God. That is happy.

SCOUT: God wants us to tell about Him.

SCAMPER: *(places ear against seashell opening)* I like this shell, Scout.

SCOUT: It's telling us how the ocean sounds!

Discussion Questions

1. How does a seashell sound?
2. Where do you find seashells?
3. What did God tell Jonah to do?
4. What happened to Jonah?
5. Can you name some animals that live in the sea?
6. Who can you tell about God?

We Can Share Good News About Jesus

Based on: Matthew 1; Luke 1—An Angel Announces Jesus' Birth
Props: Place a rolled-up newspaper next to Scout and a Bible next to Scamper.

SCOUT: Hey, Scamper! I'm in training!

SCAMPER: You are?

SCOUT: (proudly) Yep. My people are teaching me tricks.

SCAMPER: That's cool. Show me what you can do.

SCOUT: OK. I can beg. (presses front paws together and nods head)

SCAMPER: That's good, Scout! Do they give you a treat when you beg?

SCOUT: I get a doggie biscuit for every trick!

SCAMPER: How nice! What else can you do?

SCOUT: I bark when my people tell me to speak.

SCAMPER: Let me hear you bark.

SCOUT: You have to say speak, first.

SCAMPER: OK. (pauses for effect) Speak, Scout!

SCOUT: (enthusiastically) Woof, woof!

SCAMPER: (pats Scout) Good boy!

SCOUT: (proudly) I've learned something else too!

SCAMPER: What else have you learned?

SCOUT: I bring the newspaper into the house for my people.

SCAMPER: What's a newspaper?

SCOUT: This is one, right here. (points to newspaper) It has things to read.

SCAMPER: What things?

SCOUT: Whatever happened yesterday is written in it.

SCAMPER: I hope it has good news.

SCOUT: I'm sure it has some good news.

SCAMPER: I know where to find good news.

SCOUT: Where, Scamper?

SCAMPER: (points to Bible) Right here in the teacher's Bible.

SCOUT: Oh. Do you mean the story of Jesus?

SCAMPER: Yes. It tells all about Him.

SCOUT: That *is* good news!

SCAMPER: We can share the good news about Jesus.

SCOUT: Now is a good time to tell others about Jesus.

SCAMPER: It's the very best time. Jesus' birthday is coming soon!

SCOUT: (happily) Woof! Woof! Woof!

Discussion Questions

1. What new things did Scout learn?
2. How does Scout speak?
3. What good news did the angel tell to Joseph?
4. Who is Jesus' mother?
5. Where do we hear good news about Jesus?
6. Who can you tell about Jesus?

Jesus Was a Special Baby

Based on: Matthew 1; Luke 1—An Angel Brings Special News

Props: Make a small birthday hat that Scout can wear or carry in at the beginning of the script. The hat can be made from a small piece of paper rolled in the shape of a cone.

Scout:	Scamper! I have good news!
Scamper:	Tell me.
Scout:	The baby boy at our house is having a birthday.
Scamper:	When?
Scout:	Next Saturday.
Scamper:	How old will he be?
Scout:	One year old.
Scamper:	How nice.
Scout:	There will be a party in the backyard. You are invited!
Scamper:	*(surprised)* Me? I'm invited? *(bounces and claps paws)*
Scout:	Yep! Will you come?
Scamper:	I'll ask my mom, but I'm sure I can!
Scout:	Good. We'll have lots of fun!

Scamper:	Are you sure your family will let a squirrel come to the party?
Scout:	They won't care. You won't be at the table. You'll be on the ground with me.
Scamper:	OK.
Scout:	We can have all the cake that is dropped.
Scamper:	*(giggles)* With a 1-year-old, that will be a lot!
Scout:	We can run and play together while the people play games.
Scamper:	Then we will eat cake under the table!
Scout:	It will be fun!
Scamper:	I'm happy for the birthday baby.
Scout:	Me too, Scamper. He is a special baby.
Scamper:	Jesus was a special baby.
Scout:	He is still special!

Discussion Questions

1. Who was invited to the party?
2. How did Scamper show his happiness at being invited to the party?
3. Who told Mary that her baby would be the Son of God?
4. How did Joseph find out the baby's name?
5. What special news can you tell?
6. How do you show your happiness at good news?

We Are Happy Jesus Was Born

Based on: Luke 1, 2—Jesus Is Born
Props: Place a small nativity scene nearby. Spread a few small pieces of straw in or around the scene.

Scout: *(looks at nativity)* Hey, Scamper! Look at this!

Scamper: What is it?

Scout: It's straw!

Scamper: *(bends over to look)* Straw?

Scout: Yeah. It is like the straw in my doghouse.

Scamper: Yep, it is just like your straw.

Scout: It makes a cozy bed.

Scamper: I know. I've stayed overnight with you before. Remember?

Scout: I remember. It's fun when you come to stay.

Scamper: Straw makes a nice bed. That's why it is kept in barns for the animals.

Scout: I guess it keeps them warm too.

Scamper: Probably.

Scout: *(looks at nativity)* I see some animals.

Scamper: *(looks at nativity)* Uh-huh. They look happy.

Scout: I know why they are happy.

Scamper: Why?

Scout: It is Jesus' birthday!

Scamper: *(looks at nativity)* You're right, Scout! I see Mary and Joseph.

Scout: Look in the manger.

Scamper: *(looks at manger)* Baby Jesus is asleep.

Scout: *(excited)* He is sleeping on straw, just like I do!

Scamper: He is! I wonder if He is warm and cozy.

Scout: I'm sure He is. *(looks at nativity)* Look, Mary has wrapped Him in warm cloths.

Scamper: I think Mary and Joseph will sleep on the straw beside the manger.

Scout: They will rest near baby Jesus all night.

Scamper: The animals will sleep too.

Scout: Do cows and sheep snore? They might wake the baby.

Scamper: *(giggles)* Silly Scout! You are so funny! *(giggles)*

Scout: *(giggles)*

Scamper: *(thoughtfully)* I like to remember the story of baby Jesus.

Scout: Me too, Scamper. *(touches baby Jesus)* We love little Jesus.

Scamper: We are happy Jesus was born.

Discussion Questions

1. What is Scout's bed made of?
2. Who was in the barn with Jesus and His family?
3. Who was there to take care of baby Jesus when He was born?
4. Where did baby Jesus sleep?
5. Whose birthday is Christmas day?
6. How can you show your love to Jesus?

We Can Celebrate Jesus' Birth

Based on: Luke 2—A Special Baby Is Born
Props: Place a photograph of a small baby nearby.

SCAMPER: Hi, Scout!

SCOUT: Hi, Scamper. What's up?

SCAMPER: There is a baby picture here.

SCOUT: Who is the baby?

SCAMPER: I don't know. Let's ask *(teacher's name)*.

SCOUT: *(teacher's name)*, who is in the picture?

TEACHER: That is *(name of baby)*, my *(relationship to teacher)*.

SCAMPER: It is a cute baby.

SCOUT: Does the baby cry?

TEACHER: Sometimes, when *(he/she)* is hungry.

SCAMPER: How do you get the baby to stop crying?

SCOUT: I know. You give it milk to drink.

SCAMPER: You could give it some nuts to eat.

SCOUT: *(giggles)* Babies don't have teeth. They can't chew nuts!

SCAMPER: *(surprised)* Babies don't have teeth?

SCOUT: Not while they are small. After they get teeth, they could eat nuts.

SCAMPER: Babies don't have teeth? I was born with teeth!

SCOUT: Baby squirrels may have teeth, but baby people do not.

SCAMPER: Oh.

SCOUT: Babies can't walk when they are born.

SCAMPER: Really? I could walk in just a few days.

SCOUT: Babies learn to walk when they are around a year old.

SCAMPER: People babies need a lot of care, don't they?

SCOUT: Yes, they do, but they are worth it. I think *(teacher's name)* must be happy to have that baby to love.

SCAMPER: *(looks at teacher, teacher nods.)* *(She/he)* is!

SCOUT: My people were happy when their baby was born.

SCAMPER: My mother was happy when *(emphasizes)* I was born!

SCOUT: *(giggles)* I'm sure she was.

SCAMPER: Jesus used to be a baby.

SCOUT: We are happy Jesus was born. We can celebrate Jesus' birth.

SCAMPER: We could have a party to show how happy we are!

SCOUT: That's a great idea, Scamper! We'll have a party for Jesus to show that we are happy He was born.

Discussion Questions

1. Who is the baby in the photo?
2. What do Scout and Scamper want to do to show that they are happy Jesus was born?
3. What did Mary use for baby Jesus' bed?
4. How do you think Mary felt when Jesus was born?
5. Who is a baby you know?
6. How can you show that you are happy Jesus was born?

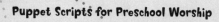

We Can Tell Others Jesus Is Special

Based on: Luke 2—Shepherds Hear Special News
Props: Place a birthday hat on Scout's head and another on Scamper's head.

SCOUT: Hi, Scamper!

SCAMPER: Hi.

SCOUT: That was some birthday party!

SCAMPER: You sure were surprised!

SCOUT: It really was a surprise birthday party!

SCAMPER: Did you have fun?

SCOUT: I did!

SCAMPER: Me too.

SCOUT: The food was great!

SCAMPER: I tried to get what everyone would like. There were seeds for the birds.

SCOUT: The ducks ate corn.

SCAMPER: All the dogs enjoyed Puppy Crunch.

SCOUT: *(puzzled)* How did you get Puppy Crunch? Did you go to the store?

SCAMPER: Animals can't go to the store, Scout.

SCOUT: Where did you get it?

SCAMPER: I took it from your bowl when you were finished eating.

SCOUT: That was smart, Scamper!

SCAMPER: Yep. I found food for everyone!

SCOUT: You must have gathered a lot of nuts for all those squirrels!

SCAMPER: *(giggles)* Lots! I didn't know what the deer family would want to eat.

SCOUT: They liked the corn!

SCAMPER: Everyone sang nicely, don't you think?

SCOUT: *(giggles)* It was a funny birthday song. The dogs howled, the ducks quacked, and the squirrels chattered!

SCAMPER: *(giggles)* It *(emphasizes)* was funny. Every animal had a different singing voice.

SCOUT: It was fun too.

SCAMPER: Everybody came.

SCOUT: I have lots of animal friends.

SCAMPER: They all think you are special!

SCOUT: They do?

SCAMPER: Of course.

SCOUT: *(hugs Scamper)* Thank you, Scamper!

SCAMPER: *(hugs Scout)* You're welcome.

SCOUT: I heard the teacher say that Jesus is special.

SCAMPER: He was a special baby. We can tell others Jesus is special.

SCOUT: *(looks at children)* We can tell the children.

SCAMPER: *(looks at children)* It will soon be Jesus' birthday.

SCOUT: I hope His birthday is as happy as mine was!

SCAMPER: Me too.

Discussion Questions

1. What was the surprise for Scout?
2. Who sang "Happy Birthday" to Scout?
3. Who told the shepherds that Jesus was born?
4. Who sang the night Jesus was born?
5. When is your birthday?
6. Who can you surprise?

We Can Tell Others Jesus Was Born

Based on: Luke 2—Shepherds Visit Jesus
Props: Place a toy sheep between Scout and Scamper.

SCAMPER: *(looks up and sees sheep)* Oh! Who are you?

SCOUT: It's a toy sheep, Scamper. Don't be afraid.

SCAMPER: *(defensively)* I'm not afraid! I was just surprised.

SCOUT: I like sheep. They are soft and cuddly.

SCAMPER: *(pets toy sheep)* You're right! It is soft.

SCOUT: I know a lot about sheep. I'm a sheepdog, you know.

SCAMPER: I know. I'm glad God made sheepdogs like you, Scout!

SCOUT: Me too. I like being a sheepdog.

SCAMPER: There are sheep in the Christmas story.

SCOUT: They were with the shepherds.

SCAMPER: I like to hear the Christmas story.

SCOUT: So do I, Scamper. I like to tell the story too.

SCAMPER: We can tell others Jesus was born.

SCOUT: The children know the story. They can tell it too.

SCAMPER: If we all tell others, soon everyone will know!

SCOUT: I like to think there were sheepdogs with the shepherds on that first Christmas.

SCAMPER: The Bible doesn't say anything about sheepdogs.

SCOUT: I know, but there *(emphasize) might* have been one.

SCAMPER: If there was one, Scout, it would have been brave, like you.

SCOUT: Yep! I am brave enough to keep sheep safe.

SCAMPER: What if a bear came?

SCOUT: Um, I guess I'm not that brave yet.

SCAMPER: When you grow up, you will be strong and brave.

SCOUT: Do you really think so?

SCAMPER: You are growing, Scout. Soon you will be bigger than me.

SCOUT: I will keep my family safe.

SCAMPER: I know something you can do right now that is brave.

SCOUT: What?

SCAMPER: You could be in the Christmas play!

SCOUT: The play could use a sheepdog!

SCAMPER: You can help tell others Jesus was born!

SCOUT: Good idea, Scamper!

Discussion Questions

1. What toy animal did Scamper pet?
2. Do you think sheepdogs were with the shepherds?
3. Who did the shepherds go to see?
4. What did the shepherds do after seeing Jesus?
5. What do you think it was like on the night Jesus was born?
6. Who can you tell about baby Jesus?

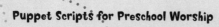

Puppet Scripts for Preschool Worship

We Are Thankful Jesus Was Born

Based on: Luke 2—Simeon and Anna See Jesus
Props: none

SCOUT: We have company at my house today, Scamper.

SCAMPER: *(curiously)* Is it another sheepdog?

SCOUT: No.

SCAMPER: Who is it?

SCOUT: The grandmother and grandfather people. They came to see the baby boy.

SCAMPER: Oh.

SCOUT: The grandfather held the baby gently in his big hands.

SCAMPER: Tell me about the grandfather.

SCOUT: He has no hair on top of his head. *(reaches paws toward top of head)*

SCAMPER: *(giggles)* Oh Scout, that is so funny!

SCOUT: *(giggles and covers mouth with paws)* I'm glad dogs don't get bald.

SCAMPER: His head must get cold in the winter!

SCOUT: Funny Scamper! He wears a hat to keep warm.

SCAMPER: *(giggles)*

SCOUT: The grandfather looked at the baby and said "thank You, God."

SCAMPER: The grandfather was happy.

SCOUT: The grandmother was happy too.

SCAMPER: How do you know?

SCOUT: She cuddled the baby in her arms. She had tears in her eyes.

SCAMPER: It sounds to me like she was sad.

SCOUT: Scamper, you don't understand. She was smiling.

SCAMPER: Couldn't she decide if she was happy or sad?

SCOUT: Silly Scamper! Sometimes there are tears when people are happy.

SCAMPER: Tell me about the grandmother.

SCOUT: She has a wrinkled face.

SCAMPER: Like the basset hound down the street?

SCOUT: *(giggles)* Not quite. Her wrinkles show when she smiles.

SCAMPER: Are the grandmother and grandfather old?

SCOUT: They look old to me.

SCAMPER: Old people love babies. They are thankful for the new baby.

SCOUT: We are thankful for all new babies.

SCAMPER: Especially for baby Jesus. We are thankful Jesus was born.

SCOUT: Jesus was a special baby.

SCAMPER: We can thank God for Jesus.

SCOUT: *Woof! Woof!*

Discussion Questions

1. Who was happy to see the new baby?
2. Who had no hair on top of his head?
3. Who had Simeon and Anna waited a long time to see?
4. What did they do when they saw baby Jesus?
5. Where do you go to worship God?
6. How can you thank God for Jesus?

We Can Worship Jesus

Based on: Matthew 2 Wise Men Worship a Special Baby
Props: none

SCAMPER: Hi, Scout!

SCOUT: Hi.

SCAMPER: I saw someone at your house.

SCOUT: The children's aunt and uncle came to visit.

SCAMPER: Oh. Did they visit you too?

SCOUT: They petted me.

SCAMPER: They like you.

SCOUT: Yes, and they love the children. They brought presents!

SCAMPER: What did they bring?

SCOUT: They gave the girl a stuffed rabbit.

SCAMPER: Did she like it?

SCOUT: Oh yes. She hugged it and carried it everywhere.

SCAMPER: She must have been happy.

SCOUT: I think so. She even read a bedtime story to the toy rabbit.

SCAMPER: Did the baby boy get a gift?

SCOUT: They brought him a musical teddy bear.

SCAMPER: Babies like music.

SCOUT: He smiled when the music played.

SCAMPER: The aunt and uncle must love the children a lot!

SCOUT: I think so. I heard them call the children "special."

SCAMPER: It's nice to be loved.

SCOUT: It sure is! I got a gift too!

SCAMPER: You did? What?

SCOUT: A squeaky toy!

SCAMPER: That sounds like fun!

SCOUT: It is. The baby and I played with it.

SCAMPER: I know another special baby.

SCOUT: Jesus?

SCAMPER: Yes. He came to earth as a baby and people gave Him gifts too.

SCOUT: They gave Him gifts to show how special He is.

SCAMPER: That's what worship is—showing Jesus how special He is.

SCOUT: We can worship Jesus.

Discussion Questions

1. Who came to visit at Scout's house?
2. Why did the baby smile?
3. Who brought gifts to Jesus?
4. How did the wise men find Jesus?
5. Who do you think is special?
6. How do you show your love to Jesus?

We Can Tell Jesus How Special He Is

Based on: Matthew 2—Wise Men Worship Jesus

Props: Prepare two tiny gift bags. Place three acorns in one bag and a dog biscuit in the other. Fasten a tiny bow to one handle of each but do not close the bags.

SCAMPER: *(holds dog biscuit bag with both paws)* Hi, Scout.

SCOUT: *(holds acorn bag with both paws)* Hi, Scamper. Did you have a nice Christmas?

SCAMPER: I sure did. How was your Christmas?

SCOUT: It was fun. My people put a new toy under the tree for me.

SCAMPER: My mother gave me some delicious seeds, but she put them *(emphasizes)* in my tree.

SCOUT: We had so much fun!

SCAMPER: *(peeks around at Scamper's bag)* Looks like you have a gift there.

SCOUT: Yep. *(peeks around at Scout's bag)* You have one too.

SCAMPER: Yep. I do.

SCOUT: Who is it for?

SCAMPER: Here, Scout. It's for you! *(sets bag next to Scout)*

SCOUT: For me? *(sets Scamper's gift down)* Thank you, Scamper! What is it?

SCAMPER: You'll see. Open it.

SCOUT: OK. I'm so excited! *(turns bag over and dog biscuit spills out)* My favorite treat! *(picks up biscuit, nibbles it, then sets it down)*

SCAMPER: I'm glad you like it, Scout.

SCOUT: *(points to unopened bag)* This one is for you, Scamper.

SCAMPER: Oh boy! I love presents! *(gently bumps bag onto its side)* Oops! *(picks up bottom end of bag and spills acorns out)*

SCOUT: Count the acorns, Scamper.

SCAMPER: *(points and counts each one)* One, two, three! Three acorns for me! Thanks!

SCOUT: You're welcome.

SCAMPER: I'll take these home to eat.

SCOUT: Christmas is fun.

SCAMPER: You know what, Scout? Jesus got gifts too.

SCOUT: I know. People gave gifts to Jesus and worshiped Him.

SCAMPER: We can worship Jesus.

SCOUT: We can worship Jesus by telling Him how special He is.

SCAMPER: He is very special.

Discussion Questions

1. Who gave Scamper a gift?
2. What was in the package for Scout?
3. Who gave gifts to baby Jesus?
4. How did the wise men worship Jesus?
5. What would you give to Jesus if you could give Him a gift?
6. How can we worship Jesus?

Jesus Pleased God

Based on: Luke 2—Jesus as a Boy
Props: none

SCAMPER: *(looks up to the top of Scout's head)* I think you are getting bigger, Scout.

SCOUT: *(looks down at self)* Do you think so?

SCAMPER: Oh yes. You are growing!

SCOUT: Did you know that grown-up sheepdogs are *(raises paws)* really big?

SCAMPER: So I've heard.

SCOUT: I'll be strong too.

SCAMPER: You will be lots stronger than me.

SCOUT: We will still be friends, even if I am bigger. *(pats Scamper)*

SCAMPER: I'm glad. *(pauses)* Am I growing bigger? *(stretches as tall as possible)*

SCOUT: I don't think so.

SCAMPER: *(hangs head)* I want to be big like you, Scout!

SCOUT: Don't be sad, Scamper. *(pats Scamper)* Squirrels are supposed to be small.

SCAMPER: I'm very small.

SCOUT: You may be small, but you are smart.

SCAMPER: Aw, Scout, you are just saying that.

SCOUT: I mean it, Scamper. That is how you have grown.

SCAMPER: *(happily)* Really?

SCOUT: You have learned a lot!

SCAMPER: I am learning more all the time.

SCOUT: Sure! You hide nuts in the ground.

SCAMPER: So?

SCOUT: You *(emphasizes)* remember where each one is hidden.

SCAMPER: Yep. I do.

SCOUT: That is very smart. *(hangs head)* Sometimes I forget where I've hidden bones.

SCAMPER: You do? *(confidently)* I never forget. Maybe I am smart, after all.

SCOUT: I am growing bigger, and my people are proud of me.

SCAMPER: My mother smiles because I've learned my squirrel lessons.

SCOUT: *(looks at children)* The boys and girls are growing and learning too.

SCAMPER: That makes their parents happy.

SCOUT: It pleases God too.

SCAMPER: Jesus grew and pleased God when He was young too.

SCOUT: God is happy when we learn and grow.

Discussion Questions

1. Who is growing?
2. What can Scamper remember?
3. How did God feel about Jesus when He was just a boy?
4. Who else was pleased with Jesus?
5. What have you learned this week that you can remember?
6. How can you please God?

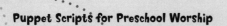

We Can Please God

Based on: Matthew 3; Mark 1—Jesus Is Baptized
Props: Fasten a cookie to Scout's paw with a rubber band.

Scamper: Hi, Scout!

Scout: *(tries unsuccessfully to cover cookie with other paw)* Huh? *(guiltily)* Oh, um, hi, Scamper.

Scamper: What have you got there?

Scout: *(looks around innocently)* Where? What are you talking about?

Scamper: In your paw! What is it?

Scout: *(removes paw covering cookie)* Oh, that? It's nothing much.

Scamper: It looks like something.

Scout: It's a cookie.

Scamper: Does it have nuts in it?

Scout: *(looks at cookie)* I think so.

Scamper: Nutty cookies are good!

Scout: Yum! I love cookies!

Scamper: Where did you get it?

Scout: *(guiltily)* Scamper, why do you ask so many questions?

Scamper: Because I'd like a cookie too.

Scout: I found it.

Scamper: Where?

Scout: *(exasperated)* If you must know, it was on my people's table.

Scamper: Uh-oh. Are you supposed to take things off of the table?

Scout: *(hangs head)* No.

Scamper: *(sternly)* Scout, you shouldn't have done that!

Scout: *(sadly)* I know.

Scamper: You made a wrong choice.

Scout: But I wanted a cookie!

Scamper: You have to put it back.

Scout: I might be in trouble.

Scamper: Maybe.

Scout: I don't know what to do.

Scamper: Maybe the children can help you decide.

Scout: *(looks at children)* What do you all think I should do? *(allow children to respond)* OK. I will put it back.

Scamper: *(pats Scout)* Good dog. You made the right choice this time.

Scout: *(looks at children)* Thank you for helping me decide.

Scamper: Children make choices too.

Scout: *(surprised)* Really?

Scamper: They can please God by doing right.

Scout: We can all choose to do right.

Scamper: We can please God.

Scout: I still want a cookie.

Scamper: I know how you can get one. Sit up and beg.

Scout: *(giggles)* Good idea, Scamper!

Discussion Questions

1. Where did Scout find the cookie?
2. What kind of cookies does Scamper like?
3. What were John's clothes made of?
4. What did Jesus do that pleased God?
5. What right choices did you make this week?
6. How can you please God?

God's Word Helps Us to Do What Is Right

Based on: Matthew 4—Jesus Is Tempted
Props: Place a Bible next to Scout and Scamper.

SCAMPER: Hi, Scout!

SCOUT: Hi, Scamper!

SCAMPER: I haven't seen you all week!

SCOUT: I've been at obedience school.

SCAMPER: What a big word! What does it mean?

SCOUT: Obedience school teaches me to obey.

SCAMPER: I thought only people went to school.

SCOUT: Nope. There are classes for dogs too.

SCAMPER: Is it fun?

SCOUT: Yes, lots of fun! I get to see other dogs.

SCAMPER: Do you play with them?

SCOUT: We play for a little while at first, then we have to learn.

SCAMPER: What did you learn?

SCOUT: I learned to walk behind my owners and not run ahead.

SCAMPER: That doesn't sound like much fun.

SCOUT: There is a reason I have to do that.

SCAMPER: Why would they want you to do that?

SCOUT: Because, Scamper, I could get hurt if I run ahead.

SCAMPER: That's true.

SCOUT: My people love me and want me to be safe.

SCAMPER: What else did you learn?

SCOUT: I learned not to jump on people.

SCAMPER: Why?

SCOUT: Because I might accidentally hurt them.

SCAMPER: A small child could fall down if you jumped on him.

SCOUT: My toenails are sharp and might scratch. *(displays bottom of foot)*

SCAMPER: *(looks at Scout's toes)* Let me see, Scout.

SCOUT: *(looking at foot)* See, they are sharp.

SCAMPER: *(feels Scout's foot with paw)* You're right, Scout!

SCOUT: Rules are good. Everyone has rules to follow.

SCAMPER: What rules do the children follow?

SCOUT: They do what their families tell them.

SCAMPER: That's good.

SCOUT: They also do what the Bible says to do.

SCAMPER: I know why. God's Word helps us do what is right.

SCOUT: God's Word is the best place to look to find out what we should do.

Discussion Questions

1. Who goes to obedience school?
2. What did Scout learn?
3. Who was tempted to eat bread?
4. What did Jesus say when He was tempted to do wrong?
5. What book tells you what is right and what is wrong?
6. What rules do you obey?

Jesus Wants Us to Tell About Him

Based on: John 1—Two Friends Follow Jesus
Props: none

SCOUT: I sure got wet! *(shakes)*

SCAMPER: Hey! *(brushes off fur)* You got water on me!

SCOUT: Oops, sorry, Scamper.

SCAMPER: I know where you've been.

SCOUT: How do you know?

SCAMPER: Every time you play at the pond, I get wet! *(giggles)*

SCOUT: I had lots of fun!

SCAMPER: What did you do at the pond?

SCOUT: I tried to play tag with some little fishes.

SCAMPER: You chased the fish?

SCOUT: Only while I was *it*.

SCAMPER: Did you tag one?

SCOUT: They were hard to catch, but I finally did.

SCAMPER: I hope you were gentle.

SCOUT: I was careful. I wouldn't hurt a fish.

SCAMPER: Did the fish play? Did it tag you?

SCOUT: *(sadly)* No, when the fish was *it,* it just swam away!

SCAMPER: *(pats Scout)* It's OK, Scout. *(pauses)* I don't think the fish knew how to play tag.

SCOUT: But I *(emphasizes)* told the fish how to play tag!

SCAMPER: Fish can't understand dog language.

SCOUT: *(giggles)* I guess you're right.

SCAMPER: *(giggles)* Did you understand the fish?

SCOUT: They didn't bark, so I don't know.

SCAMPER: You are funny, Scout! I've never heard a fish bark!

SCOUT: A barking fish? *(giggles)* That is funny!

SCAMPER: No wonder they didn't play with you.

SCOUT: *(sadly)* My barking probably scared them away.

SCAMPER: *(pats Scout)* That's OK, Scout. You can talk to the children and me.

SCOUT: *(looks at children)* Will the children run away too?

SCAMPER: Of course not. They like you.

SCOUT: *(hesitantly)* I could tell them about Jesus.

SCAMPER: Jesus wants us to tell about Him.

SCOUT: *(looks at children)* Jesus loves each of you.

SCAMPER: That's right, Scout. *(pats Scout)* Good dog!

SCOUT: *Woof! Woof!*

Discussion Questions

1. Who did Scout tag?
2. What did the fish do?
3. What did Jesus say to Nathaniel?
4. Who did Nathaniel call the Son of God?
5. Have you played tag?
6. How can you tell someone about Jesus?

Jesus Loves People Everywhere

Based on: John 4—Jesus and a Woman from Samaria
Props: none

SCAMPER: Hi, Scout!

SCOUT: Hi, Scamper. Where have you been? I looked for you.

SCAMPER: My cousins and I were running through the trees.

SCOUT: I called and you didn't answer.

SCAMPER: I didn't hear you, Scout. We went far away.

SCOUT: Oh. Where did you go?

SCAMPER: We saw a tall fence. The letters on the sign were Z-O-O.

SCOUT: That spells zoo! You went to the zoo!

SCAMPER: We jumped from one tree to another, over the fence.

SCOUT: *(dejectedly)* I haven't been to the zoo in a long time.

SCAMPER: You haven't?

SCOUT: *(sadly)* No, not since we went together.

SCAMPER: That's too bad, Scout. The zoo is fun.

SCOUT: What did you see there?

SCAMPER: Animals! Lots of animals!

SCOUT: What kinds of animals?

SCAMPER: All kinds from different countries.

SCOUT: Animals from everywhere, huh? What animals did you see?

SCAMPER: Elephants, lions, aardvarks, kangaroos. Lots of animals! They were all different sizes and colors.

SCOUT: Were there many people there?

SCAMPER: Oh yes, Scout. The people were different from one another too.

SCOUT: Maybe the people were from everywhere, just like the animals!

SCAMPER: Maybe. *(giggles)* The people and animals were looking at one another.

SCOUT: They must like seeing differences.

SCAMPER: I like animals and people who live here. I like animals and people who live in other places too.

SCOUT: It is good to be friends.

SCAMPER: God made all animals around the world. He loves them.

SCOUT: Jesus loves people everywhere too.

SCAMPER: So do I, Scout!

SCOUT: *(wistfully)* I wish I could go to the zoo again.

SCAMPER: Maybe your people will take you.

SCOUT: I hope so!

SCAMPER: You'll love it!

Discussion Questions

1. Where had Scamper been?
2. Where did the zoo animals come from?
3. What did Jesus ask the woman to do?
4. Who told the people about Jesus?
5. Can you say a word in another language? (If no one knows a word, tell the Spanish word for love, *Amor*.)
6. Who loves people everywhere?

Jesus Can Do Great Things

Based on: John 4—Jesus Heals an Official's Son
Props: Set an empty medicine bottle nearby.

SCOUT: *(sadly)* The girl at my house is sick.

SCAMPER: That's too bad, Scout.

SCOUT: She has sniffles. She sounds like this. *Sniff, sniff.*

SCAMPER: I had sniffles once. I couldn't leave the tree that day.

SCOUT: She can't go to school until she feels better.

SCAMPER: *(enthusiastically)* She must be having fun playing at home.

SCOUT: *(seriously)* No, her mother made her stay in bed today.

SCAMPER: Rest will help her get well again. It helped me when I had sniffles.

SCOUT: She has to take this medicine too *(points to bottle)*.

SCAMPER: Is it yucky?

SCOUT: I don't think so.

SCAMPER: I don't like to be sick.

SCOUT: I don't either, Scamper. It is not fun.

SCAMPER: I guess the girl is not happy.

SCOUT: She was sad.

SCAMPER: I wonder what would make her feel better?

SCOUT: I wanted to help her.

SCAMPER: What did you do?

SCOUT: I jumped onto the bed and lay beside her.

SCAMPER: That was a good idea, Scout. She wasn't alone anymore.

SCOUT: She snuggled with me and we fell asleep.

SCAMPER: You helped her to rest. *(giggles)* Did you snore?

SCOUT: *(giggles)* Funny Scamper! When we awoke, she was feeling better.

SCAMPER: I'm glad you were there, Scout.

SCOUT: Me too.

SCAMPER: Hey, Scout, I know someone else who helps sick people.

SCOUT: Who, Scamper?

SCAMPER: Jesus.

SCOUT: That's right, He makes them well.

SCAMPER: We can pray to Him when we need help.

SCOUT: He always listens to our prayers.

SCAMPER: Jesus can do great things.

Discussion Questions

1. Who had to take medicine?
2. How did Scout help the girl to feel better?
3. What did Jesus say to the father of the sick boy?
4. What did the servants tell the father?
5. Who takes care of you when you are sick?
6. Who has power to make sick people well?

We Can Tell About Jesus

Based on: Matthew 4—Jesus Begins to Teach
Props: none

SCAMPER: Hi, Scout!

SCOUT: Hi, Scamper! Let's play!

SCAMPER: Let's play school.

SCOUT: *(excited)* Animal school!

SCAMPER: I'm the teacher!

SCOUT: OK. It's your turn, anyway.

SCAMPER: *(uses his most grown-up voice and faces Scout)* All right class. Today we will learn numbers.

SCOUT: *(faces Scamper)* No fair, you know I don't know all my numbers.

SCAMPER: Then I will teach you. How many animals are in our animal school?

SCOUT: I know that. *(points at Scamper)* One, *(places paw on chest)* two.

SCAMPER: Very good, Scout. How many children are in the middle row *(or situation specific area, such as, at this table)*?

SCOUT: *(seriously)* I can do this. *(points to each child with paw, one by one)* One, two, three, *(pauses)* five, six. *(uses appropriate numbers for group if less than six)*

SCAMPER: You made a mistake, Scout.

SCOUT: *(discouraged)* I tried my best.

SCAMPER: You were right, except you left out a number.

SCOUT: Which one?

SCAMPER: Children, can you tell which number Scout forgot? *(children answer)* That's right! Four!

SCOUT: OK, four. *(takes a deep breath)* One, two, *(pauses)* four!

SCAMPER: *(looks at children)* Scout needs your help again, kids. Let's all count together. *(Scamper and children count)* One, two, three, four. Again. One, two, three, four.

SCOUT: Let me try. One, two three, *(pauses)* four! *(turns to Scamper)* Am I right?

SCAMPER: Good dog! You got every number right!

SCOUT: *(looks at children)* I did it!

SCAMPER: What good news! Who can we tell about it?

SCOUT: I'll tell my people. They like good news.

SCAMPER: The children have good news to tell too.

SCOUT: About Jesus?

SCAMPER: Yes. *(looks at children)* We can tell about Jesus.

SCOUT: We can tell friends.

SCAMPER: That was fun!

SCOUT: *(proudly)* One, two, three, four.

Discussion Questions

1. How many animals were in the animal school?
2. Who was the animal schoolteacher?
3. Who taught people about God?
4. What did Jesus do for sick people?
5. Who can you tell about Jesus?
6. What can you tell your friends about Jesus?

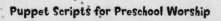

Jesus Wants Us to Obey Him

Based on: Luke 5—Fishermen Follow Jesus
Props: Set a goldfish, toy fish, or a construction paper fish in a small, clear bowl nearby.

SCAMPER: Hey, Scout, what is that?

SCOUT: It's my new pet fish!

SCAMPER: Where did you get it?

SCOUT: My people bought it at the pet store.

SCAMPER: *(looks into bowl)* It is a pretty fish.

SCOUT: *(enthusiastic)* I'm going to teach it to do tricks.

SCAMPER: Tricks? What can a fish do?

SCOUT: It will do whatever I teach it.

SCAMPER: Oh.

SCOUT: I'll tell the fish what to do, and it will obey.

SCAMPER: *(skeptical)* Are you sure?

SCOUT: Yep. I'll teach it the same tricks I learned.

SCAMPER: I want to see this.

SCOUT: OK, little fishy, lie down. *(watches fish)*

SCAMPER: I don't think it understands.

SCOUT: *(to fish)* I'll show you. *(lies down)* See? You can do it!

SCAMPER: It isn't doing what you said.

SCOUT: Come on, fishy! If you lie down, I'll give you some Puppy Crunch.

SCAMPER: *(giggles)* Fish don't eat Puppy Crunch. They eat fish food.

SCOUT: Oh. OK, I'll give you some fish food.

SCAMPER: *(looks at fish)*

SCOUT: Come on, fishy. You can do it. Lie down.

SCAMPER: I don't think it is going to obey you.

SCOUT: *(sadly)* Why not?

SCAMPER: Maybe fish don't lie down. I think they just swim.

SCOUT: Oh.

SCAMPER: I know who *(emphasizes) can* obey.

SCOUT: I can!

SCAMPER: You can, *(looks at children)* and the children can too.

SCOUT: Jesus wants us to obey Him.

SCAMPER: Children know how to obey.

SCOUT: Fish don't.

SCAMPER: *(looks at fish)* It is a nice fish, Scout.

SCOUT: *(looks at fish)* He is a very good fish, even if he can't do tricks.

Discussion Questions

1. Who has a fish?
2. What won't the fish do?
3. Where did Jesus stand when He talked to the people?
4. How did Jesus help the disciples?
5. Have you ever caught a fish?
6. How can you obey Jesus?

Jesus Can Always Help Us

Based on: Mark 2; Luke 5—Jesus Heals a Man Who Could Not Walk
Props: Place a small bucket over Scout's head.

SCOUT: Scamper! Where are you?

SCAMPER: I'm here, Scout. *(looks at Scout and giggles)* You are funny, Scout!

SCOUT: No, it's not funny! I can't get out.

SCAMPER: Just push it off with your paws.

SCOUT: *(puts paws on bucket)* Errr . . . oof! It won't come off!

SCAMPER: How did you get your head into that bucket?

SCOUT: It was in the trash.

SCAMPER: Dogs do not belong in the trash.

SCOUT: I know. But I wanted the crumbs inside the bucket.

SCAMPER: What kind of crumbs?

SCOUT: Puppy treats came in this bucket. The crumbs are yummy.

SCAMPER: Oh. *(pauses and looks at Scout)* You are in a mess.

SCOUT: What am I going to do, Scamper?

SCAMPER: Let's think and come up with a plan.

SCOUT: Think fast! I want out now!

SCAMPER: I know! I'll pull it off.

SCOUT: OK, Scamper. *(bends head in opposite direction of Scamper)*

SCAMPER: Hey, I'm over here!

SCOUT: *(turns toward Scamper)* I can't see where you are.

SCAMPER: Right here. Don't move. *(places front paws on bucket and grunts)* Errr, it is on tight!

SCOUT: I know. Try again.

SCAMPER: *(places paws on bucket and grunts more loudly)* Errr! It won't come off, Scout.

SCOUT: Oh dear, I want a drink! I can't even get a drink!

SCAMPER: *(soothingly)* Calm down, Scout. I'll think of something.

SCOUT: Get help!

SCAMPER: That's what I'll do. Will *(call a child by name)* please help? *(Scamper and child pull the bucket off Scout's head)*

SCOUT: *(to child and Scamper)* Whew! Thank you. I'm glad to have helpful friends.

SCAMPER: You're welcome.

SCOUT: Do you know who else always helps?

SCAMPER: I do. Jesus can always help us.

SCOUT: If we ask, He hears and answers us.

Discussion Questions

1. What happened to Scout?
2. How did Scamper help?
3. How did the sick man's friends help him?
4. What did Jesus do for the sick man?
5. Who can you ask when you need help?
6. How have you helped a friend?

Jesus Loves All People

Based on: Matthew 9; Luke 5—Jesus and Matthew
Props: Show a picture of a raccoon.

SCOUT: *(cheerily)* Good morning, Scamper.

SCAMPER: *(grumpily)* Hi, Scout.

SCOUT: Is something wrong, Scamper?

SCAMPER: *(emphatically) Something* is very wrong!

SCOUT: What happened?

SCAMPER: Some of my corn is gone!

SCOUT: Did you eat it?

SCAMPER: Not me. That bad, old raccoon ate it while I was sleeping.

SCOUT: How do you know the raccoon did it?

SCAMPER: I heard noises in the night. I peeked out to see who it was.

SCOUT: You saw the raccoon eating?

SCAMPER: Yes.

SCOUT: Did the raccoon see you?

SCAMPER: No, some barking dogs scared it away.

SCOUT: You are brave, Scamper. Raccoons are lots bigger than you.

SCAMPER: *(proudly)* I am brave. *(pauses)* I wonder why the raccoon stole my corn?

SCOUT: I think it was just hungry.

SCAMPER: *(angrily)* The raccoon is a thief! It was wearing a mask!

SCOUT: *(giggles)* Silly Scamper! That's just the color of its fur.

SCAMPER: *(puzzled)* Really?

SCOUT: Yes, really. There is darker fur around its eyes. See, I have darker fur on my ear tips. *(tilts head so Scamper can see)*

SCAMPER: *(looks at Scout's ear)* It is darker. The raccoon is different than us.

SCOUT: You *(points to Scamper)* are different than I *(points to self)* am.

SCAMPER: *(looks at Scout, then looks down at self)* You're right! We're not the same.

SCOUT: Jesus loves all animals. He even loves raccoons.

SCAMPER: Does Jesus love people too?

SCOUT: Of course He does.

SCAMPER: How about your family?

SCOUT: I'm sure He loves them.

SCAMPER: *(thoughtfully)* People are not all the same.

SCOUT: The children here are not all the same.

SCAMPER: Does Jesus love all of them?

SCOUT: Jesus loves them, every one.

SCAMPER: *(happily)* Jesus loves raccoons and children.

SCOUT: *(points to children)* Jesus loves you, *(points to Scamper)* and Scamper, *(points to self)* and me.

Discussion Questions

1. Who ate Scamper's corn?
2. Who did Scout say Jesus loves?
3. When Jesus asked Matthew to follow Him, what did Matthew do?
4. Who had dinner with Matthew?
5. How are people different from one another?
6. Does Jesus only love some people? Who does He love?

We Can Do What Pleases God

Based on: Matthew 5–7—Jesus Teaches About Pleasing God
Props: none

SCAMPER: *(indignantly)* Scout, did you see that?

SCOUT: No, what?

SCAMPER: That bird stole my bread crumbs!

SCOUT: It did?

SCAMPER: It flew really fast and grabbed the bread from my paws!

SCOUT: *(impressed)* Wow! What a quick bird!

SCAMPER: *(irritated)* Hey, whose side are you on anyway?

SCOUT: Um, *(pauses)* I didn't know I had to be on someone's side.

SCAMPER: *(sternly)* Well, are you my friend or not?

SCOUT: Scamper, of course I'm your friend.

SCAMPER: Then you are on *(emphasizes)* my side.

SCOUT: I didn't know it was a fight. I don't want to fight a bird.

SCAMPER: *(exasperated)* That bird took my food!

SCOUT: I guess it was hungry.

SCAMPER: I'm hungry too, Scout!

SCOUT: I know what to do.

SCAMPER: Yeah, so do I! I just might punch that bird out!

SCOUT: *(pats Scamper)* Settle down. There's a better way.

SCAMPER: I can't think of anything else to do.

SCOUT: I have lots of bread in my bowl.

SCAMPER: Why aren't you guarding it?

SCOUT: Why should I?

SCAMPER: That bird will take your food too!

SCOUT: I don't care. I have enough for all three of us.

SCAMPER: You do?

SCOUT: Yep. I'll share with you *(emphasizes) and* the bird!

SCAMPER: That's nice of you, Scout. Why would you share with that mean bird?

SCOUT: I don't think the bird is mean. It's just hungry.

SCAMPER: *(calmer)* Oh. Maybe it does need food, just as I do.

SCOUT: Everyone needs food.

SCAMPER: OK, we can share with someone who doesn't have food.

SCOUT: Sure we can. We can do what pleases God.

SCAMPER: God? Uh-oh. I had forgotten that we should help others.

SCOUT: *(looking up)* Come here, bird! We have food for you!

SCAMPER: Come on bird, we will share!

Discussion Questions

1. Who took Scamper's bread?
2. What did Scout do for the bird?
3. Where did the people follow Jesus?
4. Who does Jesus say we should love?
5. How can you show love to your friends?
6. Who can you pray for?

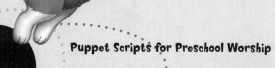

Give to God

Based on: Matthew 6; Mark 12—Jesus Teaches About Giving
Props: none

SCAMPER: *(wearily)* Hi, Scout.

SCOUT: Hey, Scamper, where have you been?

SCAMPER: I was in the woods.

SCOUT: Does your mother know you went there?

SCAMPER: Yes, she does.

SCOUT: Are you sure?

SCAMPER: *(sternly)* Scout, you know that squirrels play in the woods all the time!

SCOUT: Oh, yeah.

SCAMPER: Anyway, all the big squirrels look out for us little ones.

SCOUT: I forgot about that.

SCAMPER: I have a secret in the woods.

SCOUT: You do? What is it?

SCAMPER: If I tell, it won't be a secret.

SCOUT: Tell me! I won't tell anyone.

SCAMPER: Nope.

SCOUT: *(pleading)* Please, Scamper!

SCAMPER: I guess I could give you a hint.

SCOUT: *(eagerly)* Yes, give me a hint! I'll try to guess!

SCAMPER: It is something to get ready for spring.

SCOUT: Hm. Are you planting flowers?

SCAMPER: Nope. It is too early for that.

SCOUT: I give up.

SCAMPER: I took twigs and leaves from my nest to the woods.

SCOUT: Why?

SCAMPER: That's the secret!

SCOUT: *(eagerly)* Tell me, Scamper! I've got to know!

SCAMPER: All right, but don't tell the birds. It is a surprise.

SCOUT: I won't tell.

SCAMPER: I piled it all under the trees.

SCOUT: For the birds?

SCAMPER: Yes. Now they won't have to fly and search. Everything they need to build a nest is there.

SCOUT: But Scamper, won't you be cold? You gave up your nest!

SCAMPER: Maybe just a little. I'll have to snuggle up.

SCOUT: Why would you give up your nest?

SCAMPER: I wanted to give to God.

SCOUT: *(puzzled)* But you said it was for the birds!

SCAMPER: It is. That is how we give to God. By helping others.

SCOUT: The birds will be happy!

SCAMPER: Yep. They might even chirp a happy song!

Discussion Questions

1. What was Scamper's secret?
2. What did Scamper give to the birds?
3. How much did the widow put in the offering?
4. Who did Jesus say gave all she had?
5. Who gives you food and clothes?
6. What can you give to help someone?

Jesus Has Power to Heal People

Based on: Matthew 8; Luke 7—Jesus Heals the Soldier's Servant
Props: Attach a bandage to Scamper's knee.

SCAMPER: Ouch!

SCOUT: What's wrong, Scamper?

SCAMPER: My knee hurts. I scraped it on the sidewalk.

SCOUT: How did it happen?

SCAMPER: I was in the tree and . . .

SCOUT: *(interrupts)* There are no sidewalks in trees!

SCAMPER: *(giggles)* Funny Scout!

SCOUT: But you said you were in the tree.

SCAMPER: I was, but I slipped and fell onto the sidewalk.

SCOUT: That's a long way to fall, Scamper.

SCAMPER: Yeah, it is.

SCOUT: Sidewalks are rough.

SCAMPER: I know.

SCOUT: Does it hurt?

SCAMPER: A little.

SCOUT: Did you cry?

SCAMPER: Nope.

SCOUT: You were brave not to cry.

SCAMPER: *(proudly)* I'm getting big. I don't cry *(emphasizes)* every time I fall.

SCOUT: Oh. *(pauses)* Do you have a bandage?

SCAMPER: Uh-huh. *(moves front paw so Scout can see knee)* See?

SCOUT: *(looks at bandage)* Is it all better now?

SCAMPER: Not yet. I have to keep the bandage on all day.

SCOUT: Will it be better tomorrow?

SCAMPER: Probably. My mom put medicine on it.

SCOUT: Medicine helps scrapes to get better.

SCAMPER: Bandages keep hurt places clean.

SCOUT: Mothers know how to help us.

SCAMPER: I'm glad my mom took care of my knee.

SCOUT: Your knee will get well now, Scamper.

SCAMPER: I know.

SCOUT: One day, the girl at my house fell off her bike.

SCAMPER: Was she hurt?

SCOUT: She needed a bandage on her arm.

SCAMPER: Did she get well?

SCOUT: She is as good as new.

SCAMPER: Jesus helps people get well when they are hurt or sick.

SCOUT: Jesus has power to heal people.

SCAMPER: Tomorrow I'll be climbing trees again!

SCOUT: *(giggles)* You'd better be careful!

SCAMPER: *(giggles)* I will, Scout. I'll hang on very tightly!

Discussion Questions

1. How did Scamper get hurt?
2. What will make Scamper better?
3. What was wrong with the soldier's helper?
4. What did Jesus do for the soldier's helper?
5. Does a bandage make you feel better when you are hurt?
6. Who can make us well when we are sick?

Jesus Always Cares for Us

Based on: Luke 7—Jesus Brings a Young Man Back to Life
Props: none

Scout: Hi, Scamper!

Scamper: Hi, Scout. I was just at your house and you weren't there.

Scout: I was at the neighbor's house.

Scamper: Why?

Scout: My people went away for the day.

Scamper: So?

Scout: I'm only a little puppy and someone has to take care of me.

Scamper: They left you with a puppy sitter?

Scout: Yep.

Scamper: Did you like being there?

Scout: It was fun. I played with other puppies.

Scamper: Why didn't your people leave you home alone?

Scout: They love me very much. They want me to be safe.

Scamper: I don't ever stay with a squirrel sitter.

Scout: Don't your parents want you to be safe?

Scamper: Sure they do. All the grown-up squirrels look out for us young ones.

Scout: How do you know which one to mind?

Scamper: I have to mind any squirrel that gives the signal.

Scout: What is the signal?

Scamper: If there is danger, squirrels swish their tails like this. *(swishes tail)* That is the signal.

Scout: How do you know what that means?

Scamper: All little squirrels learn to stand very still if they see a tail swish.

Scout: You can run and play without worrying because the grown-up squirrels are watching out for you.

Scamper: That's right, Scout.

Scout: My family is different from yours.

Scamper: They sure are.

Scout: Our families are the same in other ways.

Scamper: They are? How?

Scout: They make sure we are safe. They love us.

Scamper: They do, don't they? Families are caring.

Scout: They all care in their own way.

Scamper: Don't forget, Scout, that Jesus cares too.

Scout: I know. Jesus always cares for us.

Discussion Questions

1. Who took care of Scout?
2. How are Scout's and Scamper's families the same?
3. Why was the mother sad?
4. What did Jesus do for the son?
5. Who takes care of you when the adults in your family are away?
6. Who will always care for you?

Jesus Has Power to Stop a Storm

Based on: Mark 4—Jesus Stops a Storm
Props: none

SCAMPER: What's wrong, Scout?

SCOUT: *(breathless)* I went to the pond to play, but I was afraid!

SCAMPER: I'm the one who is afraid at the pond.

SCOUT: This time, I was.

SCAMPER: Why?

SCOUT: There were waves!

SCAMPER: That's because the wind was blowing.

SCOUT: Wind makes waves, all right.

SCAMPER: I thought you liked the water.

SCOUT: I like it when it is still. I don't like the water splashing high.

SCAMPER: I don't like that either.

SCOUT: What about the fish? I hope the fish are OK.

SCAMPER: *(giggles)* Fish are at home in the water.

SCOUT: I know, but are fish afraid when the waves are big?

SCAMPER: When the wind blows my tree, it rocks my nest. Maybe the water rocks the fish in the same way.

SCOUT: That sounds like fun for the fish.

SCAMPER: Don't worry about them.

SCOUT: The turtles might get splashed.

SCAMPER: Turtles enjoy being splashed!

SCOUT: Are you sure?

SCAMPER: They like it! I've seen them sitting on a log in the sunshine with the water splashing on them.

SCOUT: I'm glad to hear that. What about frogs?

SCAMPER: *(giggles)* Frogs like to dive.

SCOUT: There is a *(emphasizes)* big splash when a frog jumps into the water!

SCAMPER: *(giggles)* They like splashing in water.

SCOUT: I have lots of pond friends.

SCAMPER: God cares for all the animals. They are safe.

SCOUT: *(timidly)* I guess I was the only one who was afraid.

SCAMPER: It's OK, Scout. God cares when we are afraid.

SCOUT: Jesus has power to stop a storm.

SCAMPER: He does, and He can help us when we are afraid.

SCOUT: *(braver)* I'm not afraid anymore.

Discussion Questions

1. Why was Scout afraid?
2. Who cares for fish, turtles, and frogs?
3. Why were the disciples afraid?
4. What did Jesus do to help them?
5. Who helps you to not be afraid?
6. How can we ask God to help us?

Jesus Has Power to Help Families

Based on: Luke 8—Jesus Heals a Young Girl
Props: none

SCOUT:	Guess what happened, Scamper!
SCAMPER:	Tell me.
SCOUT:	The baby in our family was lost!
SCAMPER:	Oh no!
SCOUT:	The parents looked in the house.
SCAMPER:	Did they find him there?
SCOUT:	No. They looked in the yard next.
SCAMPER:	Was he there?
SCOUT:	Nope. They couldn't find him anywhere!
SCAMPER:	What did the parents do?
SCOUT:	They were very upset.
SCAMPER:	Did the police come?
SCOUT:	Nope. The father said, "Scout, find the baby!"
SCAMPER:	He needed your help.
SCOUT:	It was an important job.
SCAMPER:	Did you think you could help?
SCOUT:	Yes, because dogs have a way of finding things.
SCAMPER:	How?
SCOUT:	Dogs have good noses. They can smell things that people cannot.
SCAMPER:	You could smell the baby?
SCOUT:	I could smell where he had been.

SCAMPER:	How can that help?
SCOUT:	All I had to do was follow the trail.
SCAMPER:	You are smart, Scout!
SCOUT:	*(modestly)* Thanks, Scamper. I just sniffed *(sniff, sniff)* around the floor where he had been playing.
SCAMPER:	Did you pick up the scent?
SCOUT:	Yep. I followed his trail through the kitchen, past the living room, and into the bedroom.
SCAMPER:	Was he there?
SCOUT:	I found him asleep under the bed!
SCAMPER:	Didn't the people look there?
SCOUT:	They looked *(emphasizes) in* the bed but not under it. Covers were hanging down and they didn't see him.
SCAMPER:	How did you tell the family you found him?
SCOUT:	I barked and they came.
SCAMPER:	*(impressed)* You are a hero!
SCOUT:	*(proudly)* I got a lot of praise and petting!
SCAMPER:	You helped the family!
SCOUT:	Do you know who else helps families? Jesus has power to help families.
SCAMPER:	Jesus?
SCOUT:	Yep. Jesus has power to help families.

Discussion Questions

1. Who was lost?
2. Who helped the family find the baby?
3. Who did the girl's father ask for help?
4. What did Jesus do for the girl and her family?
5. How many people are in your family?
6. How has Jesus helped your family?

JeSUS Has Power to Give Us What We Need

Based on: John 6—Jesus Feeds a Crowd
Props: Place a small, unbreakable dish next to Scout.

SCOUT: *(eating from dish)* Mmmm. *(wiping mouth with paw)* I ate almost all of my dinner. It was good!

SCAMPER: *(holding stomach)* I'm hungry too! What did you have to eat?

SCOUT: My favorite—Puppy Crunch! Do you want some? *(pushing dish toward Scamper)*

SCAMPER: *(looking into dish then turning away)* Dog food? No, thank you.

SCOUT: Why not?

SCAMPER: *(pushing dish back to Scout)* Yuk! I don't like dog food. I only eat nuts.

SCOUT: *(looking at dish)* Does your owner put nuts in a bowl for you?

SCAMPER: No. I don't have an owner.

SCOUT: Then how are you fed?

SCAMPER: God knows that we need food. *(pointing up)* He made acorns grow on trees for squirrels.

SCOUT: I'm glad God takes care of animals.

SCAMPER: Yes, He loves all living things. Jesus has power to give us what we need.

SCOUT: He must be special to know what *(spreading front paws)* everyone needs.

SCAMPER: He cares for all of us—animals *(pointing to self)*, and *(pointing to children)* people too!

SCOUT: *(looking at children)* People too?

SCAMPER: *(nodding head)* Jesus knows what they need. He cares for every one of them.

SCOUT: *(looking at children)* I hope they remember to say thank You to Jesus.

SCAMPER: Me too! Come on Scout, let's play!

TEACHER: Scout had a great idea! Let's all fold our hands and bow our heads while we thank Jesus. Thank you, Jesus, for knowing what we need. Thank you for giving us good food. Amen.

Discussion Questions

1. Who wanted to share lunch today?
2. Who made Scamper's lunch in the trees?
3. What did the boy share in the Bible story?
4. What special thing did Jesus do at lunchtime?
5. Where does your food come from?
6. What do we say to Jesus for giving us good things to eat?

JeSUS Has Power to Walk on Water

Based on: Mark 6; John 6—Jesus Walks on Water
Props: none

Scout: Hey, Scamper, guess where I've been playing! *(shakes to dry fur)*

Scamper: That's not hard to guess. *(wipes face with paws)* You shook pond water all over me!

Scout: Oh. Sorry, Scamper.

Scamper: It's OK, Scout. My fur will dry. *(smoothes belly fur with paw)*

Scout: I saw lots of things at the pond!

Scamper: What did you see?

Scout: I saw a bunch of happy tadpoles! They were wiggling all over.

Scamper: What is a tadpole?

Scout: Scamper, haven't you ever seen a tadpole?

Scamper: I don't think so. Do they live in trees?

Scout: You are funny. *(giggles)* Tadpoles live in water.

Scamper: What do they look like?

Scout: They have big heads and cute tails.

Scamper: Oh. What do they do?

Scout: They wiggle their tails to swim. They grow up to be frogs.

Scamper: *(skeptical)* You can't fool me, Scout! Frogs don't have tails.

Scout: Not frogs, but tadpoles do. When their legs grow, their tails disappear.

Scamper: *(giggles)* God must have smiled when He made them.

Scout: *(giggles)* I guess He did!

Scamper: What else did you see?

Scout: I saw fish, turtles, and a little snake.

Scamper: Lots of animals live in the water.

Scout: There was a duck that floated on top of the water.

Scamper: That would be fun! Did you float too?

Scout: *(giggles)* Dogs can't float.

Scamper: Squirrels can't either.

Scout: I wonder if any other animals can float?

Scamper: I don't know. I know of someone who can walk on water.

Scout: I don't think so, Scamper.

Scamper: Yes I do. It's in the Bible!

Scout: Really? Who?

Scamper: Jesus. Jesus has power to walk on water.

Scout: That's amazing!

Scamper: Jesus is God's Son. He can do anything!

Discussion Questions

1. What did Scout see at the pond?
2. What animal begins life as a tadpole?
3. Who can walk on water?
4. Who saw Jesus walk on water?
5. What is an animal that floats on the water?
6. What animals live in the water?

Jesus Can Help Us Because He Is the Son of God

Based on: Mark 7—Jesus Heals a Man Who Could Not Hear or Speak
Props: none

SCOUT: *(paws over ears)*

SCAMPER: What are you doing, Scout?

SCOUT: *(removes paws from ears)* What did you say, Scamper? I couldn't hear you.

SCAMPER: Why did you have your ears covered?

SCOUT: I wanted to see what it is like to not hear.

SCAMPER: Some people cannot hear.

SCOUT: I know. They talk with their hands. It is called sign language.

SCAMPER: Squirrels sign with their tails.

SCOUT: Really, Scamper? You know sign language?

SCAMPER: I don't know people's sign language. I only know the squirrel sign for danger.

SCOUT: Show me the sign that squirrels give.

SCAMPER: *(turns and shakes tail)*

SCOUT: That's good, Scamper.

SCAMPER: Show me a sign that people do.

SCOUT: OK. I know how to sign love. *(cross arms over chest)*

SCAMPER: Let me try, Scout! *(cross arms over chest)* I did it!

SCOUT: That's right, Scamper!

SCAMPER: Let's do another!

SCOUT: I know one more. It means happy. *(pats chest several times with front right paw)*

SCAMPER: I can do that! *(pats chest several times with front left paw)*

SCOUT: Try again, Scamper. This time use your right paw.

SCAMPER: Huh? *(looks at both paws)* Oh, I used my left. *(pats chest several times with front right paw)*

SCOUT: You've got it now. You learned two signs today!

SCAMPER: If I meet someone who cannot hear, I can say love *(cross arms over chest)* and I can say happy. *(pats chest several times with front right paw)*

SCOUT: Yes, you can.

SCAMPER: Jesus helps people who cannot hear.

SCOUT: Jesus can help us because He is the Son of God.

SCAMPER: We praise Jesus because He does everything well.

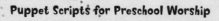

Discussion Questions

1. What did Scout do to shut out the noise?
2. What did Scout teach Scamper?
3. What happened to the man who could not hear?
4. Who is God's Son?
5. Who can help us?
6. How can you talk to people who cannot hear?

JeSUS Has Power to Help People

Based on: John 9—Jesus Heals a Man Born Blind
Props: Place a black Bible nearby. Locate a yellow object in the room for later use in this script.

SCAMPER:	Let's play a game!
SCOUT:	OK. What shall we play?
SCAMPER:	The color game is fun.
SCOUT:	OK. You go first.
SCAMPER:	*(looks around)* I see something reddish brown!
SCOUT:	*(looks around)* Is it *(name of a child who is wearing brown shoes)*'s shoes?
SCAMPER:	Nope. Guess again!
SCOUT:	Is it your tail?
SCAMPER:	You guessed it! Your turn, Scout!
SCOUT:	I see something white.
SCAMPER:	*(looks around)* Is it *(name of a child who is wearing a white shirt)*'s shirt?
SCOUT:	*(excited)* No.
SCAMPER:	*(looks at tummy)* I know! Is it my tummy fur?
SCOUT:	Nope. It is a fluffy cloud I saw while coming to church!
SCAMPER:	No fair! It has to be something in this room.
SCOUT:	Oh. OK. Why don't you go next?
SCAMPER:	OK. *(looks around)* I see something black.
SCOUT:	*(looks around)* Is it *(name of child with dark hair)*'s hair?
SCAMPER:	Nope.
SCOUT:	Is it *(looks at Scamper)* your nose?

SCAMPER:	Nope!
SCOUT:	My nose?
SCAMPER:	Nope.
SCOUT:	*(looks around and sees Bible)* I know! *(excited)* It is the Bible!
SCAMPER:	You guessed it, Scout!
SCOUT:	The Bible tells about Jesus helping people.
SCAMPER:	Jesus has power to help people.
SCOUT:	He helps everyone who asks Him.
SCAMPER:	Your turn, Scout.
SCOUT:	*(looks around)* I see something yellow.
SCAMPER:	*(looks around)* Is it *(name of yellow object in classroom)*?
SCOUT:	Nope.
SCAMPER:	*(looks around)* Scout, I don't see anything else that is yellow.
SCOUT:	It is *(name of blonde child)*'s hair!
SCAMPER:	That's not yellow! It's blonde.
SCOUT:	It is?
SCAMPER:	You need to practice your colors. I'll help you.
SCOUT:	You help me. Who helps people?
SCAMPER:	Jesus has power to help people.
SCOUT:	*(points to Bible)* The Bible says so.

Discussion Questions

1. What game did Scout and Scamper play?
2. What did Scamper see that was black?
3. How long had the man been blind?
4. How did Jesus help him?
5. What color is your shirt/dress?
6. How many colors can you name?

We Can Help Others

Based on: Matthew 7; Luke 10—Jesus Teaches About Helping
Props: none

SCAMPER: Scout, guess what happened!

SCOUT: *(curious)* What?

SCAMPER: I found it under my tree.

SCOUT: What did you find?

SCAMPER: A baby mole.

SCOUT: What's a mole?

SCAMPER: It's a small animal.

SCOUT: What does it look like?

SCAMPER: It is like a mouse, only fatter.

SCOUT: *(giggles)* A fat mouse?

SCAMPER: Yes, and it has a very short tail.

SCOUT: Mice have *(emphasize)* long tails.

SCAMPER: Moles have soft, warm, fur coats.

SCOUT: That's good. They can keep warm in winter.

SCAMPER: This mole was lost.

SCOUT: Oh.

SCAMPER: He was scared.

SCOUT: *(sympathetic)* Poor baby.

SCAMPER: I helped him to go home.

SCOUT: Where do moles live?

SCAMPER: They live in tunnels underground.

SCOUT: Really?

SCAMPER: Yes.

SCOUT: Did you go underground to find his home?

SCAMPER: *(giggles)* Squirrels don't like to be under the ground!

SCOUT: Then how did you take him home?

SCAMPER: I looked around and found where the tunnels were.

SCOUT: *(with admiration)* You are smart, Scamper!

SCAMPER: *(modestly)* It was easy.

SCOUT: How did you get him inside?

SCAMPER: I went to the end of the tunnel and made a door by digging!

SCOUT: Squirrels are good diggers.

SCAMPER: The mole family was inside, watching.

SCOUT: What did the baby mole do when he saw his family?

SCAMPER: He quickly scrambled inside.

SCOUT: What happened next?

SCAMPER: I shut the door.

SCOUT: *(skeptical)* How do you shut a hole in the ground?

SCAMPER: The same way you open it, by digging! Only this time, my tail was toward the door. The dirt flew back and covered the end of the tunnel.

SCOUT: *(impressed)* Wow, Scamper, you knew just what to do!

SCAMPER: I was happy to help.

SCOUT: We can help others.

Discussion Questions

1. Who was lost?
2. What did Scamper do for the baby mole?
3. How does Jesus want us to treat others?
4. What did the Samaritan do for the hurt man?
5. Who can you help?
6. What nice thing can you do for someone?

Puppet Scripts for Preschool Worship

JeSUS Wants Us to Learn About Him

Based on: Luke 10—Mary and Martha Follow Jesus
Props: Place a cookie nearby.

SCOUT: Hi, Scamper!

SCAMPER: Hi, Scout. *(looks at cookie)* What is that?

SCOUT: It's a cookie. The girl at my house made it.

SCAMPER: Really?

SCOUT: Yep. The mother is teaching her to cook.

SCAMPER: How nice.

SCOUT: The girl had fun. I watched. I licked up the crumbs that spilled.

SCAMPER: You had fun too.

SCOUT: I did.

SCAMPER: How do you make cookies?

SCOUT: Pour lots of sugar into a *(emphasizes)* big bowl.

SCAMPER: Sugar makes cookies sweet.

SCOUT: Put in eggs and nuts and other stuff.

SCAMPER: What other stuff?

SCOUT: I don't know. I was on the floor and couldn't see everything.

SCAMPER: What did they do next?

SCOUT: The girl stirred until she was tired.

SCAMPER: It must be a hard job.

SCOUT: The mother finished the stirring.

SCAMPER: But how does all that mess turn into cookies?

SCOUT: They put small pieces of the dough on pans and cooked them in the oven.

SCAMPER: Were they cookies then?

SCOUT: Hot cookies! They had to wait for them to cool.

SCAMPER: Then they gave you one?

SCOUT: I got two, one for me and one for you.

SCAMPER: *(looks at cookie)* I only see one.

SCOUT: I ate mine. *(rubs stomach)* It was yummy!

SCAMPER: This one is mine?

SCOUT: Yep.

SCAMPER: Thank you, Scout! I love cookies with nuts in them!

SCOUT: You're welcome.

SCAMPER: *(nibbles at cookie)* The girl learned how to make *(emphasizes)* good cookies.

SCOUT: She sure did!

SCAMPER: *(looks at children)* Have these children learned to make cookies?

SCOUT: Some of them have. They've learned other things as well.

SCAMPER: At church?

SCOUT: Yes. Jesus wants us to learn about Him.

SCAMPER: They are learning *(emphasizes)* very well!

Discussion Questions

1. Who learned to cook?
2. What did Scout give to Scamper?
3. Who cooked a meal for Jesus?
4. Why didn't Mary help cook?
5. Who cooks at your house?
6. Who teaches you about Jesus?

God Always Hears Our Prayers

Based on: Matthew 6; Luke 11—Jesus Teaches About Praying
Props: Print a note in large letters that says, "Dear Scamper, Come play with me tomorrow. Love, Scout."

SCAMPER: *(holding note between paws)* I got your note, Scout!

SCOUT: Read it!

SCAMPER: *(looks at note)* "Dear Scamper, Come play with me tomorrow. Love, Scout."

SCOUT: *(delighted)* You read it and you came!

SCAMPER: Uh-huh. I did.

SCOUT: I like to get letters.

SCAMPER: Me too, Scout.

SCOUT: We could send letters every day!

SCAMPER: That would be fun.

SCOUT: Scamper, if we are sending letters to each other, we won't be together.

SCAMPER: *(pauses)* I like to be with you, Scout.

SCOUT: I like being with you too.

SCAMPER: I want to be here. I don't want to be home alone.

SCOUT: I'd rather talk to you than write a note.

SCAMPER: OK. We will just talk.

SCOUT: Let's talk about having fun.

SCAMPER: We do have lots of fun.

SCOUT: We play games.

SCAMPER: We run together.

SCOUT: We eat table scraps together sometimes.

SCAMPER: *(rubs stomach)* Yum.

SCOUT: I tell you everything!

SCAMPER: Because we are best friends!

SCOUT: I like to talk to you, Scamper.

SCAMPER: Who else talks to you?

SCOUT: My family talks to me.

SCAMPER: What do they say?

SCOUT: Usually they say, "good dog!"

SCAMPER: *(pats Scout)* You are a good dog.

SCOUT: Thanks. My family talks to God too.

SCAMPER: Talking to God is called prayer.

SCOUT: I know.

SCAMPER: *(looks at children)* These children can talk to God.

SCOUT: *(looks at children)* We can pray to God. God always hears our prayers.

TEACHER: What a good idea, Scout! *(looks at children)* Let's talk to God.
God, we are glad that we can talk to you anytime. We can tell You everything. You will always hear us and love us. Amen.

Discussion Questions

1. Who wrote a note to Scamper?
2. What do Scout and Scamper like to talk about?
3. Who do we talk to when we pray?
4. Who taught the disciples how to pray?
5. What do you talk about with your family?
6. What can you say to God?

We Can Share with Others

Based on: Luke 12—Jesus Teaches About Sharing
Props: Place a small container full of dry dog food between Scout and Scamper.

SCAMPER: *(looks at dog food)* Wow, Scout, what a lot of food!

SCOUT: I don't think I can eat that much!

SCAMPER: You might get sick if you eat it all.

SCOUT: I don't want to get sick.

SCAMPER: Eat as much as you want. Save the rest for later.

SCOUT: It might spoil if it is left over.

SCAMPER: What will you do with all of it?

SCOUT: Do you want some?

SCAMPER: Yuk! I don't like Puppy Crunch!

SCOUT: I forgot.

SCAMPER: I have a great idea!

SCOUT: What?

SCAMPER: You can share with another dog.

SCOUT: I don't know any other dogs.

SCAMPER: I don't either.

SCOUT: Maybe we can call and one will come.

SCAMPER: Good idea! Here, dog! *(pats paws together)* Come on, boy!

SCOUT: Here dog! Free food! Come here, girl!

SCAMPER: *(surprised)* No one came. *(looks around)*

SCOUT: *(disappointed)* I don't see a dog anywhere. *(looks around)*

SCAMPER: We could put the food out on the sidewalk. A dog might pass by.

SCOUT: I'm not allowed to drag my dish away.

SCAMPER: Oh. Can you think of anything else to do with it?

SCOUT: We might throw it in the trash.

SCAMPER: You would be in trouble for sure when the flies start buzzing around!

SCOUT: I guess I'll just leave it here to waste.

SCAMPER: That's too bad.

SCOUT: I'm sure there is a dog somewhere.

SCAMPER: Hey, I remember now!

SCOUT: What?

SCAMPER: A little dog was resting under my tree.

SCOUT: *(excited)* Get him, Scamper. I'll let him eat some Puppy Crunch!

SCAMPER: I'm on my way!

SCOUT: We can share with others.

Discussion Questions

1. What did Scout have to share?
2. What was Scamper's idea?
3. What was the rich man's plan?
4. What did God want the rich man to do?
5. Who shares with you?
6. What can you share with a friend?

Jesus Is God's Son

Based on: John 11—Jesus Brings Lazarus Back to Life
Props: none

SCOUT: Scamper!

SCAMPER: *(pops up)* Here I am, Scout.

SCOUT: *(hugs Scamper)* I'm glad we are friends.

SCAMPER: *(hugs Scout)* Me too!

SCOUT: We have fun, don't we?

SCAMPER: We sure do!

SCOUT: Remember when we had a sleepover in my doghouse?

SCAMPER: That was fun!

SCOUT: Except when I got scared.

SCAMPER: *(giggles)* It was just an owl saying, *"Whoo!"*

SCOUT: *(giggles)*

SCAMPER: How about when we played hide-and-seek?

SCOUT: You couldn't find me under the porch.

SCAMPER: I looked and looked for you.

SCOUT: I came out when you called me.

SCAMPER: Yep.

SCOUT: I like when we play animal school.

SCAMPER: I am always the teacher.

SCOUT: That's because you are ahead of me and know more.

SCAMPER: I like teaching you to count.

SCOUT: Don't forget the ABCs!

SCAMPER: You've learned *(emphasizes)* most of them.

SCOUT: *(sadly)* I still get mixed up on *L, N, M, O, P.*

SCAMPER: *(giggles)* You sure do! Don't worry. I'll help you learn.

SCOUT: What else do we do that is fun?

SCAMPER: We come to church!

SCOUT: It is lots of fun to learn about Jesus!

SCAMPER: Jesus is God's Son.

SCOUT: *(looks at children)* We learn with the children!

SCAMPER: Do you know what else I like to do with you, Scout?

SCOUT: *(curious)* What?

SCAMPER: I like when you share your bread with me.

SCOUT: You look cute sitting up nibbling bread from your paws.

SCAMPER: *(giggles)* Do I?

SCOUT: I know what I like best! I like to race with you, Scamper.

SCAMPER: You do, huh? Catch me! *(scampers away)*

SCOUT: Here I come! *(runs after Scamper)*

Discussion Questions

1. Who is Scout's best friend?
2. What do Scout and Scamper like to do together?
3. What friend did the sisters ask for help?
4. What did Jesus do for His friend Lazarus?
5. Who is your best friend?
6. What games do you and your friend like to play?

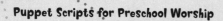

Jesus can Make Sick People Well

Based on: Luke 17—Jesus Heals 10 Men
Props: Tie a bandage on Scout's front paw.

SCAMPER: Hi, Scout. Let's play!

SCOUT: *(sadly)* Not today, Scamper.

SCAMPER: Why not? Are you sick?

SCOUT: I hurt my foot. *(holds bandaged paw toward Scamper)* See?

SCAMPER: *(looks at Scout's paw)* What happened?

SCOUT: I stepped on a thorn.

SCAMPER: Ouch! That must have hurt!

SCOUT: It did!

SCAMPER: *(looks at bandage)* Who fixed it?

SCOUT: My owner. He pulled the thorn out.

SCAMPER: Did you cry?

SCOUT: Yes. I really howled!

SCAMPER: *(pats Scout sympathetically)* Poor Scout.

SCOUT: After the thorn was gone, he washed my foot.

SCAMPER: That gets the dirt out so it can get well.

SCOUT: I know. He put on medicine too.

SCAMPER: That will help your paw to heal.

SCOUT: I want it to get better.

SCAMPER: Your owner cares for you.

SCOUT: He held me and petted me until I quit howling.

SCAMPER: Why do you have a bandage?

SCOUT: That is to keep it clean.

SCAMPER: *(pats Scout)* It will get well now.

SCOUT: Yep.

SCAMPER: People and animals have bodies that can get well.

SCOUT: God thought of everything. He makes our hurts heal.

SCAMPER: Jesus can make sick people well.

SCOUT: *(looks at children)* Children too?

SCAMPER: All people.

SCOUT: God cares for people, just like my owner cares for me.

SCAMPER: Hey Scout, I have an idea!

SCOUT: What?

SCAMPER: We can play a quiet game.

SCOUT: One where we don't run?

SCAMPER: Sure. We can play school.

SCOUT: You be the teacher.

SCAMPER: OK. I'll have you count to 10.

SCOUT: I might get mixed up a little.

SCAMPER: That's OK. The teacher will help you.

Discussion Questions

1. What happened to Scout?
2. Who took care of Scout?
3. What did Jesus do for the sick people?
4. What did the healed man say to Jesus?
5. Who takes care of you when you are sick?
6. Who makes our bodies well?

Jesus Loves Children

Based on: Mark 10—Jesus and the Children
Props: Set a toy car, cup, and saucer nearby.

SCOUT: Hey, Scamper, where were you?

SCAMPER: I was playing in the trees with my cousins.

SCOUT: What kind of games do squirrels play?

SCAMPER: Sometimes we play tag.

SCOUT: I've noticed you squirrels like to chase one another.

SCAMPER: It's fun!

SCOUT: Puppies like to chase too.

SCAMPER: Do you play tag?

SCOUT: Not exactly. We chase and tumble.

SCAMPER: What kind of game is that?

SCOUT: It's not really a game. We just tumble over one another.

SCAMPER: Don't you have rules?

SCOUT: Nope. It is fun to just play!

SCAMPER: When I see puppies playing together, they get all jumbled up.

SCOUT: *(giggles)* We sure do! What else do squirrels play?

SCAMPER: I taught my cousins to play follow the leader.

SCOUT: That is fun!

SCAMPER: *(thoughtfully)* Scout, I'm wondering, what do children play?

SCOUT: The little boy at my house likes to play cars.

SCAMPER: I'm scared of cars. They are big!

SCOUT: He plays with toy cars *(puts paw on car)* like this one. He pushes them along *(slightly push car with paw)* and says *vroom!*

SCAMPER: What does the girl play?

SCOUT: She plays house.

SCAMPER: Does she pretend to be a house?

SCOUT: *(giggles)* Silly Scamper! She pretends to be the mother.

SCAMPER: How does she do that?

SCOUT: She dresses her baby doll and feeds it a toy bottle.

SCAMPER: What else does she do?

SCOUT: She pretends to cook dinner for her teddy bears.

SCAMPER: *(giggles)* Do the teddy bears pretend to eat?

SCOUT: The girl pretends they are eating. Each one has a plate and a cup *(points with paw)* like these.

SCAMPER: Children and animals like to play.

SCOUT: Jesus loves children.

SCAMPER: He loves us all.

Discussion Questions

1. What games do squirrels play?
2. How are squirrels, dogs, and children alike?
3. Who did the people ask to bless their children?
4. How did Jesus show His love to children?
5. How can you show your love to other children?
6. Who have you shown love to?

Jesus Wants Us to Follow Him

Based on: Luke 18; Mark 10—Bartimaeus Follows Jesus
Props: none

SCOUT: *(has paws over eyes)*

SCAMPER: Hi, Scout.

SCOUT: Where are you, Scamper? I can't see you.

SCAMPER: Silly Scout, take your paws off your eyes, then you can see.

SCOUT: *(removes paws from eyes)* There you are!

SCAMPER: Why did you have your eyes covered?

SCOUT: I wanted to hide.

SCAMPER: You can't hide like that.

SCOUT: Sure I can, see? *(covers eyes with paws)* I'm gone! You can't see me.

SCAMPER: Yes I can.

SCOUT: I can't see anything.

SCAMPER: You can't see me.

SCOUT: Nope.

SCAMPER: I can see you.

SCOUT: *(puzzled; removes paws from eyes)* You can? How?

SCAMPER: Like this. *(covers eyes with paws)* I can't see you now.

SCOUT: You can't? I see you.

SCAMPER: *(uncovers eyes)* I see you now.

SCOUT: How'd you do that?

SCAMPER: *(giggles)* Cover your eyes, Scout.

SCOUT: *(covers eyes with paws)* I don't see you, Scamper.

SCAMPER: Right.

SCOUT: *(uncovers eyes)* Now I do!

SCAMPER: If you cover your eyes, you are the one who can't see.

SCOUT: Awesome! I get it!

SCAMPER: I'm glad I can see.

SCOUT: Me too, Scamper.

SCAMPER: It can be fun to hide your eyes in a game.

SCOUT: Like hide-and-seek?

SCAMPER: Yes.

SCOUT: I like hide-and-seek.

SCAMPER: We can play it after church if you want.

SCOUT: *(excited)* OK, let's do!

SCAMPER: Right now, we'll learn with the boys and girls.

SCOUT: What are we supposed to learn today?

SCAMPER: We'll learn more about Jesus.

SCOUT: OK.

SCAMPER: Jesus wants us to follow Him.

SCOUT: How can kids do that if they can't see Jesus?

SCAMPER: They can do what He said they should do.

SCOUT: Oh. Like being nice to others?

SCAMPER: Exactly!

SCOUT: Let's go play now.

SCAMPER: OK!

Discussion Questions

1. Why couldn't Scout see Scamper?
2. What game does Scout like to play?
3. What did the man want Jesus to do for him?
4. What did Bartimaeus do after Jesus healed him?
5. What do you like to see with your eyes?
6. How can you follow Jesus?

Jesus Wants Us to Love Others

Based on: Luke 19—Jesus and Zacchaeus
Props: none

SCOUT: *(happily)* Hi, Scamper!

SCAMPER: Hi, Scout.

SCOUT: Let's play.

SCAMPER: OK. What game do you want to play?

SCOUT: We always play tag. Let's play something different.

SCAMPER: Like what?

SCOUT: Let's play tumble. It's my favorite puppy game.

SCAMPER: *(doubtful)* Um, I don't know, Scout. I've seen puppies tumbling and it looks rough.

SCOUT: It's fun. You'll see! *(reaches paw to Scamper)* Come on.

SCAMPER: *(pauses)* Tell me how to play.

SCOUT: Easy. We just tumble around together. *(reaches paw to Scamper)* Come on.

SCAMPER: *(doubtfully)* Well, *(pauses)* OK.

SCOUT: *(quickly wrestles Scamper down)* See, I told you it is fun!

SCAMPER: *(grunting)* I'll get you now, Scout! *(wrestles Scout down)*

SCOUT: Here I come. Get ready! *(pushes Scamper off)*

SCAMPER: *(tries to grab Scout)* Oh no you don't. You won't get away!

SCOUT: *(places mouth on Scamper's paw)* Grrr.

SCAMPER: Ouch! *(jerks away from Scout and looks at paw)* You bit me!

SCOUT: *(cheerfully)* Isn't this fun? Let's do it again!

SCAMPER: *(emphatically)* No, Scout!

SCOUT: Why not?

SCAMPER: I don't like being bit! *(looks at paw)* I'm not playing anymore.

SCOUT: But Scamper, that is how puppies play. We growl and nip one another as we tumble.

SCAMPER: *(indignantly)* I'm not a puppy. I don't like it.

SCOUT: *(looks at Scamper's paw repentantly)* Did I hurt you?

SCAMPER: A little.

SCOUT: *(sincerely)* I'm so sorry, Scamper! *(loudly kisses Scamper's paw)* There. Is it all better?

SCAMPER: Much better, Scout.

SCOUT: I love you, Scamper. You are my friend.

SCAMPER: I know, Scout.

SCOUT: Jesus wants us to love others.

SCAMPER: Yep. And we do. We're forever friends!

SCOUT: Let's play something else.

SCAMPER: OK. *(tags Scout)* You're *it!*

Discussion Questions

1. Why didn't Scamper want to play tumble?
2. Who was sorry for biting?
3. Why couldn't Zacchaeus see Jesus?
4. What did Zacchaeus climb?
5. What should you do if someone accidentally hurts you?
6. How can you show love to someone?

We Can Praise Jesus

Based on: Matthew 21—A Crowd Welcomes Jesus
Props: none

SCAMPER: Hi, Scout! *(hugs Scout)*

SCOUT: *(hugs Scamper)* Hi! I'm happy to see you. *(looks at children)* We're glad to see you kids too!

SCAMPER: We love coming to church!

SCOUT: That's right, Scamper.

SCAMPER: The grown-ups are happy to see each other too.

SCOUT: Why do you think that?

SCAMPER: They all smile and shake hands.

SCOUT: How do you shake hands?

SCAMPER: Here, I'll show you. *(holds out right paw)* Now take my paw with your right paw.

SCOUT: *(puts right paw against Scamper's right paw)* Like this?

SCAMPER: You've got it! Now shake hands! *(moves paw up and down)*

SCOUT: *(moves paw in sync with Scamper's paw)* Like this?

SCAMPER: Uh-huh. We just shook hands.

SCOUT: *(puzzled)* Why do people do that?

SCAMPER: It is a way to greet people and make them feel welcome.

SCOUT: *(giggles)* That is funny, Scamper!

SCAMPER: *(giggles)* It's funny if you are an animal. Animals have other ways of saying hello.

SCOUT: Dogs sniff *(sniff, sniff)* and touch noses. *(touches nose to Scamper's)*

SCAMPER: *(giggles)* When squirrels meet, they chase one another for fun.

SCOUT: Birds tweet hello. *(high-pitched)* Tweet, tweet!

SCAMPER: Cats rub against people's legs.

SCOUT: The neighbor cat rubs against my fur.

SCAMPER: That means the cat likes you.

SCOUT: I think so. It is a nice cat.

SCAMPER: All the people at church smile as they talk to one another.

SCOUT: I think that means they are glad to be together.

SCAMPER: They make one another feel welcome.

SCOUT: How can we make Jesus feel welcome at our church?

SCAMPER: We can praise Jesus.

SCOUT: Jesus is welcome here. I am welcome too.

SCAMPER: The children like us.

SCOUT: Ooh, *(shivers)* I feel good all over!

SCAMPER: So do I, Scout! It's good to be loved.

Discussion Questions

1. How did Scout and Scamper welcome one another?
2. How do people welcome one another?
3. What did the disciples bring for Jesus to ride?
4. How did the people make Jesus feel welcome?
5. Who welcomes you in church?
6. How can you welcome a visitor?

We Can Celebrate Jesus

Based on: Mark 11—People Praise Jesus
Props: none

SCAMPER: What was all the noise this morning?

SCOUT: What noise?

SCAMPER: I heard sirens and music.

SCOUT: Oh, that. It was a parade. I saw it. It was fun!

SCAMPER: What's a parade?

SCOUT: A parade starts with the fire truck and police cars.

SCAMPER: I was afraid of the sirens.

SCOUT: Noise won't hurt you. It is exciting.

SCAMPER: I covered my ears and hid.

SCOUT: I covered my ears and barked.

SCAMPER: What else did you see?

SCOUT: The school band was marching. They played music.

SCAMPER: Wow! I wish I'd seen that.

SCOUT: The scouts carried flags.

SCAMPER: I'm going to the next parade! Tell me more.

SCOUT: The parade people threw candy to children.

SCAMPER: Did they throw any acorns?

SCOUT: *(giggles)* Silly Scamper!

SCAMPER: Oh well, I like candy too.

SCOUT: You should have seen the big horses.

SCAMPER: Animals were in the parade?

SCOUT: Animals, clowns, and bicycles were all in the parade.

SCAMPER: That sounds like fun.

SCOUT: There were cars too. Important people rode in them.

SCAMPER: Why do people have parades?

SCOUT: It was a celebration! A brave soldier came home.

SCAMPER: Was the parade for him?

SCOUT: It was. He waved and smiled at everyone.

SCAMPER: His family must have been happy.

SCOUT: The whole town is glad. He is a hero.

SCAMPER: Everyone loves a hero.

SCOUT: Everybody cheered for him.

SCAMPER: He deserves a big celebration.

SCOUT: I know someone else who is a hero.

SCAMPER: Who, Scout?

SCOUT: Jesus.

SCAMPER: That's right. He deserves our praise.

SCOUT: People celebrated when Jesus came to their town.

SCAMPER: Cheering is a way to celebrate Jesus.

SCOUT: We can celebrate Jesus. *(loudly)* Yay Jesus!

SCAMPER: That is right, Scout. Jesus is our hero.

Discussion Questions

1. What noise did Scamper hear?
2. Who was the most important person in the parade?
3. What did Jesus ride on when people cheered for Him?
4. What did the people wave in the air?
5. Who is God's Son?
6. How can you celebrate Jesus being alive?

Jesus Is Alive!

Based on: Matthew 27, 28—Jesus Is Alive!
Props: Bring a blooming springtime plant in a pot with top of its bulb exposed above the soil. Also bring a dry bulb.

SCAMPER: *(holds dry bulb between paws)*

SCOUT: Hi, Scamper! What do you have?

SCAMPER: I have a flower bulb.

SCOUT: What's it for?

SCAMPER: It's for you! It will grow into a flower.

SCOUT: *(skeptical)* Aw, Scamper. You can't fool me!

SCAMPER: I'm serious, Scout!

SCOUT: *(looks at bulb)* I don't see how that thing can make a flower!

SCAMPER: God makes it happen.

SCOUT: OK, I want to see Him do it right now.

SCAMPER: *(sets bulb down)* He doesn't just do it suddenly. He has a plan.

SCOUT: A plan?

SCAMPER: Yes. First, the bulb must be planted in the ground or in a pot of dirt.

SCOUT: *(understanding)* Like when you plant a seed?

SCAMPER: Yes. Next, it needs water.

SCOUT: Rain?

SCAMPER: If it is outside, it will get rain. If it's inside, you have to water it.

SCOUT: I see.

SCAMPER: It needs sunshine too.

SCOUT: What if it is inside in a pot? There's no sun indoors.

SCAMPER: You put it by a window where the sun can shine through.

SCOUT: Then does it come alive?

SCAMPER: Yep! Soon you see a tiny green sprout.

SCOUT: *(excited)* It will be fun to watch!

SCAMPER: It is! We see lots of plants and trees coming alive in the spring.

SCOUT: I saw some flowers on my way to church today!

SCAMPER: The whole world looks happy!

SCOUT: What will my plant look like when it blooms?

SCAMPER: *(points to blooming potted plant)* It will look like that one.

SCOUT: *(looks at plant)* It is very pretty, Scamper.

SCAMPER: I'm glad to see everything come alive in the springtime. It reminds me of Jesus.

SCOUT: Jesus is alive!

Discussion Questions

1. What surprise did Scamper give to Scout?
2. What makes the bulb grow into a flower?
3. Why were Jesus' friends sad?
4. What made them happy again?
5. When do flowers come alive?
6. What do you like about springtime?

Puppet Scripts for Preschool Worship

We Are Happy Jesus Is Alive

Based on: John 21—Jesus Lives!
Props: Hang a picture of a butterfly nearby.

SCAMPER: Remember the little worm that lived on my tree last summer?

SCOUT: I remember. It was a fat, green worm.

SCAMPER: It was cute. I liked that worm.

SCOUT: How can you be friends with a worm?

SCAMPER: We sat on a limb together and watched the clouds.

SCOUT: That worm is lucky to have you for a friend.

SCAMPER: Thank you, Scout. I have lots of friends.

SCOUT: What happened to that worm, anyway?

SCAMPER: When the weather got cold, it hid in a cocoon. I was sad. We couldn't play anymore.

SCOUT: Did the worm die during the cold winter.

SCAMPER: No! It's alive, Scout!

SCOUT: *(skeptical)* Are you sure?

SCAMPER: Yes.

SCOUT: How do you know?

SCAMPER: I was sitting on the limb, looking at the cocoon.

SCOUT: Because you missed your friend?

SCAMPER: I did. *(excited)* I saw the cocoon move, Scout!

SCOUT: What happened?

SCAMPER: I kept watching and it wiggled.

SCOUT: *(skeptical)* Cocoons can't wiggle.

SCAMPER: This one did! Then it tore the cocoon on the end.

SCOUT: Oooh! Gross!

SCAMPER: *(irritated)* Now listen to this, Scout!

SCOUT: What?

SCAMPER: Next, a head came out. It was my worm friend!

SCOUT: Really?

SCAMPER: Uh-huh. But the worm had changed.

SCOUT: How did it change?

SCAMPER: It is now a butterfly like this one. *(points to butterfly picture)* It's still my friend.

SCOUT: Awesome!

SCAMPER: I am so glad that my friend is alive!

SCOUT: That is good news, Scamper!

SCAMPER: I was sad, but now I am happy because my friend is alive!

SCOUT: Jesus' friends were sad when they did not see Him anymore.

SCAMPER: They were happy when He came back.

SCOUT: We are happy Jesus is alive!

Discussion Questions

1. Where did the worm hide?
2. What came out of the cocoon?
3. Who came back to life?
4. Who saw Jesus while fishing?
5. What makes you happy?
6. What good news can you tell?

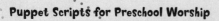

We Can Follow Jesus

Based on: Acts 2—The Church Begins
Props: none

SCAMPER: Hi, amigo!

SCOUT: What? I can't understand you.

SCAMPER: Amigo. I said amigo.

SCOUT: What is an *amigo?*

SCAMPER: It means "friend." You are my friend.

SCOUT: Oh. Where did you learn that word?

SCAMPER: It is Spanish. I know words in two languages.

SCOUT: I wish I could speak two languages. I speak dog language, but I can't understand cat words at all.

SCAMPER: Silly Scout! *(giggles)* Spanish and English are people languages.

SCOUT: *(admiringly)* You are so smart, Scamper.

SCAMPER: Thank you, Scout.

SCOUT: Do you know another Spanish word?

SCAMPER: I can say three more words, *uno, dos, tres.*

SCOUT: Hey, I learned those words on a TV puppet show! Uno, dos, tres!

SCAMPER: Do you know what they mean?

SCOUT: Sure I do. One, two, three!

SCAMPER: See, you do know words in another language!

SCOUT: I'm smart like you, amigo.

SCAMPER: *(giggles)* Yep.

SCOUT: *(looks at children)* Can you kids count to three in Spanish? *(children answer)* Some of you must watch the same TV show that I do.

SCAMPER: *(looks at children)* I want to hear you all count.

SCOUT: OK, *(looks at children)* everybody count, *(children count with Scout)* uno, dos, tres.

SCAMPER: *(watches children)* You kids are smart too!

SCOUT: I heard some people talking in another language.

SCAMPER: What did they say?

SCOUT: I don't know. I don't understand their language.

SCAMPER: Another one? How many languages are there?

SCOUT: All places in the world have their own languages.

SCAMPER: Wow! That must be about a kazillion languages!

SCOUT: Jesus loves people of all languages and wants them to follow Him.

SCAMPER: We can follow Jesus.

SCOUT: That's right, amigo!

Discussion Questions

1. What does *amigo* mean?
2. What words can Scamper say in Spanish?
3. In what language did the people hear Peter speak?
4. What did the people do after they learned about Jesus?
5. What words can you say in another language?
6. What language is spoken in your home?

We Can Share with Friends at Church

Based on: Acts 2, 4—The Church Follows Jesus
Props: Place a coloring book and two large red and blue crayons next to Scout and Scamper.

SCOUT:	*(holds red crayon between paws and colors on one page)* I am coloring a dog!
SCAMPER:	*(holds blue crayon between paws and colors other page)* I am coloring a flower!
SCOUT:	Oops! I got out of the lines a little!
SCAMPER:	*(looks at Scout's page)* It's not that bad.
SCOUT:	*(looks at Scamper's page)* You color nicely. You got outside the lines only once.
SCAMPER:	Thank you, Scout. Yours is good too.
SCOUT:	This is a *(emphasizes) big* red dog!
SCAMPER:	Mine is a nice blue flower.
SCOUT:	*(lays down red crayon)* I am going to give my dog a blue collar.
SCAMPER:	*(continues to color)*
SCOUT:	*(loudly)* I said, I want to color a blue collar for my dog.
SCAMPER:	I heard you.
SCOUT:	Then why aren't you giving me the blue crayon?
SCAMPER:	Because I'm using it.
SCOUT:	I need it *(emphasizes) now!*

SCAMPER:	*(irritated)* You can't have it!
SCOUT:	*(reaches toward blue crayon)* Give it to me!
SCAMPER:	*(continues to hold blue crayon)* I had it first!
SCOUT:	I'll tell the teacher!
SCAMPER:	Tattletale!
TEACHER:	What is going on here?
SCAMPER:	Scout tried to take my crayon! It's mine!
SCOUT:	I need blue, and Scamper won't let me have it.
TEACHER:	Remember what we learned about sharing?
SCAMPER:	*(ashamed)* I guess I forgot.
SCOUT:	*(embarrassed)* I was trying to remember.
TEACHER:	Try again, and remember to share.
SCAMPER:	*(meekly)* I'm sorry, Scout. *(lays down crayon)* You can use the blue.
SCOUT:	*(timidly)* I'm sorry too, Scamper.
SCAMPER:	It is more fun to share than to argue.
SCOUT:	We can share with friends at church.
SCAMPER:	*(hugs Scout)* We are friends.
SCOUT:	*(hugs Scamper)* We will share.

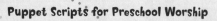

Discussion Questions

1. What are Scout and Scamper doing at church?
2. How did Scout and Scamper solve their argument?
3. What did the friends do with their money?
4. What else did the disciples share?
5. Who shares dinner at your house?
6. What can you share with a friend?

We Learn About Jesus from Other People

Based on: Acts 3—Peter and John at the Temple
Props: none

SCAMPER: *(panting)* Whew! That was a fast race!

SCOUT: *(panting)* You were fast, Scamper!

SCAMPER: So were you, Scout! I had to run very fast to beat you.

SCOUT: You win this time.

SCAMPER: Maybe next time you can win.

SCOUT: I'll try. My legs are getting bigger and stronger every day.

SCAMPER: I have strong legs because I climb trees a lot.

SCOUT: I can do lots of things with my legs.

SCAMPER: What can you do?

SCOUT: I can run. I can jump *(jumps)*. I can swim in the pond.

SCAMPER: I can run and jump too.

SCOUT: We are growing.

SCAMPER: Just like the children.

SCOUT: *(looks at children)* I think the girls and boys are getting strong.

SCAMPER: I know they are. Look at *(insert a male child's name)*. He had a birthday this month.

SCOUT: He is bigger than at his last birthday.

SCAMPER: His legs are strong. When he is a man, he will have much longer legs!

SCOUT: So will we when we are grown, Scamper. Little animals and little people grow to be bigger.

SCAMPER: Our minds are growing too, Scout.

SCOUT: I know a lot of things. I can count to six!

SCAMPER: *(looks at children)* The children are learning too.

SCOUT: *(insert a female child's name)* has learned to tie her shoes!

SCAMPER: She couldn't do that last year.

SCOUT: I know why the children come to church.

SCAMPER: To learn?

SCOUT: Yes, to learn about Jesus.

SCAMPER: The teacher tells stories about Him.

SCOUT: I like the stories.

SCAMPER: Me too!

SCOUT: We are all learning new things about Jesus.

SCAMPER: We learn about Jesus from other people.

SCOUT: I'm glad we have someone to teach us.

SCAMPER: Me too.

Discussion Questions

1. Who won the race?
2. Why are Scamper's legs strong?
3. Why didn't the man work for his food?
4. What did Peter and John do for the man?
5. What can you do with your legs?
6. Who tells you about Jesus?

We Learn About Jesus from the Bible

Based on: Acts 8—Philip Tells About Jesus
Props: none

Scamper: You've been gone three days. I missed you.

Scout: I was on a trip with my people.

Scamper: A trip?

Scout: Yes. We traveled far away in the car.

Scamper: Going far away sounds exciting.

Scout: It was. I watched out the window until I was tired. Then I took a nap on the car floor.

Scamper: Where did you go?

Scout: We visited the grandmother and grandfather.

Scamper: Was it fun?

Scout: It was lots of fun.

Scamper: What did you eat while you were there?

Scout: Mostly, I ate Puppy Crunch. I ate food scraps under the table too.

Scamper: What did you do while you were there?

Scout: I played in the yard with the children.

Scamper: What else did you do?

Scout: We all walked on the beach. I wore my collar and leash.

Scamper: I've never been to the beach.

Scout: You'd like it, Scamper. I watched birds dive for fish.

Scamper: Wow!

Scout: I saw boats.

Scamper: Did you go on a boat?

Scout: No, but lots of them were traveling on the water.

Scamper: What else did you do?

Scout: I snuggled at the grandmother's feet. She read a bedtime story to the children.

Scamper: What storybook did she read from?

Scout: A children's Bible storybook.

Scamper: Really?

Scout: Yes. The very best stories come from the Bible.

Scamper: We learn about Jesus from the Bible.

Scout: The children listened to the stories, then fell asleep.

Scamper: Where did you sleep?

Scout: They put a pillow on the floor for me to sleep on.

Scamper: How cozy!

Scout: We came home yesterday.

Scamper: I'm glad you are home, Scout.

Scout: I missed you too, Scamper.

Discussion Questions

1. Where did Scout go in the car?
2. What stories did the grandmother read to the children?
3. Who told Philip where he should go?
4. What book was the man reading?
5. What book tells about Jesus?
6. Do you have a Bible of your own?

We Can Do What Jesus Wants Us to Do

Based on: Acts 9—Saul Begins to Follow Jesus

Props: Cover a quarter-sized cardboard circle with aluminum foil. Punch a hole in the circle and thread a ribbon through the hole. Hang the ribbon around Scout's neck.

Scamper: Hey, Scout! What is that? *(places paw on silver tag)*

Scout: I got it for finishing my lessons at obedience school.

Scamper: You mean you are out of school?

Scout: I am for now.

Scamper: You must have done well.

Scout: *(proudly)* I did.

Scamper: Did all the dogs get a medal?

Scout: No. Some have to go back.

Scamper: You are smart, Scout.

Scout: Thank you. I learned it all in the first term!

Scamper: How did you learn so much?

Scout: I just followed directions!

Scamper: Whose directions?

Scout: My owner's and the teacher's.

Scamper: What things did you learn at dog obedience school?

Scout: I learned to speak.

Scamper: *(looks at children)* Speak for us, Scout.

Scout: You have to say speak first.

Scamper: *(looks at children)* Kids, tell Scout to speak. *(wait for children to respond)*

Scout: *Woof! Woof!*

Scamper: *(pats Scout)* Good dog! What else did you learn?

Scout: I can sit, lie down, and be quiet.

Scamper: Anything more?

Scout: Lots more! I can fetch.

Scamper: What does fetch mean?

Scout: If my owner tells me to fetch and throws a ball, I run to get it.

Scamper: Why?

Scout: It's a game. Sometimes I fetch the newspaper too.

Scamper: You do lots of things.

Scout: I learned how to do what my owner wants me to do.

Scamper: The children can do what they're supposed to do too.

Scout: They can?

Scamper: They can do what Jesus wants them to do.

Scout: *Woof! Woof!*

Scamper: You did great, Scout!

Discussion Questions

1. Who is out of school?
2. What has Scout learned?
3. What surprised Saul as he walked down the road?
4. Who told Ananias to go to Saul?
5. Whose rules do you follow?
6. What does Jesus want you to do?

God Wants Us to Tell Others About Jesus

Based on: Acts 9—Peter and Tabitha
Props: none

SCAMPER:	Hi, Scout!
SCOUT:	*(dejected)* Hi, Scamper.
SCAMPER:	What's wrong, pal?
SCOUT:	The girl in my family is going to kindergarten.
SCAMPER:	That's good, Scout. She is old enough to learn at school.
SCOUT:	I'll miss her.
SCAMPER:	Yes, but it won't be long each day until she comes home.
SCOUT:	She's learning the alphabet.
SCAMPER:	She'll soon learn to read.
SCOUT:	I want to learn too.
SCAMPER:	You can do it. I'll help you.
SCOUT:	You will? Can we start now?
SCAMPER:	Sure. The first three letters are *A, B,* and *C.*
SCOUT:	*A, B, C.*
SCAMPER:	*(pats Scout)* Good, dog. That's right. Now say *D, E, F.*
SCOUT:	*D, E, F.*
SCAMPER:	That's the way! Now say them all together, *A, B, C, D, E, F.*
SCOUT:	*A, B, (pauses) D, E, F.*

SCAMPER:	You only forgot one. Try again, *A, B, (emphasizes) C, D, E, F.*
SCOUT:	*A, B, C, D, E, F.*
SCAMPER:	You can say six letters of the alphabet!
SCOUT:	You are a good friend, Scamper. You helped me to learn.
SCAMPER:	*(looks at children)* The children are learning at church.
SCOUT:	The teacher helps them learn about Jesus.
SCAMPER:	We can help too.
SCOUT:	Are you sure, Scamper?
SCAMPER:	I'm sure. We can help others learn about Jesus.
SCOUT:	God wants us to tell others about Jesus.
SCAMPER:	Yep. Now, let me hear you say the first six letters of the alphabet.
SCOUT:	Um, *(pauses) A, B, (pauses) C* is what I missed last time. *C. (hangs head)* I don't remember what comes next.
SCAMPER:	*D, E, F.* You almost had it.
SCOUT:	*A, B, C, D, E, F.*
SCAMPER:	Practice these and I'll teach you the next six letters tomorrow.
SCOUT:	OK. *A, B, C, D, E, F.*

Discussion Questions

1. What is Scout learning?
2. Who helped Scout to learn?
3. Why were Tabitha's friends crying?
4. What was Peter's surprise for Tabitha's friends?
5. Who are the church helpers?
6. How can you help someone learn about Jesus?

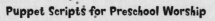

We Can Pray for People Who Tell About Jesus

Based on: Acts 12—The Church Prays for Peter in Prison
Props: none

SCAMPER: Hey, Scout. I saw lots of people in church today.

SCOUT: You did?

SCAMPER: I did! I climbed a tree outside the window.

SCOUT: What did you see?

SCAMPER: I saw children in a class, like this one.

SCOUT: What did they do?

SCAMPER: They listened to the teacher and answered questions.

SCOUT: *(looks at children)* Just like these children!

SCAMPER: Yep. When they finished with the lesson, the children got to make things with paper, crayons, and paste.

SCOUT: That sounds like fun!

SCAMPER: I think so. They were smiling.

SCOUT: What else did you see, Scamper?

SCAMPER: I saw big people through another window.

SCOUT: What were they doing?

SCAMPER: The teacher was reading from a Bible. Everyone was listening.

SCOUT: I didn't know that big people needed a teacher.

SCAMPER: I guess everyone needs to learn more about the Bible.

SCOUT: What else happened?

SCAMPER: I heard a buzzer! *(making a buzzing sound) Buzzz!* It was loud!

SCOUT: I can do that too. *(making a buzzing sound) Buzzz!* What was the buzzer for?

SCAMPER: I think it meant that class was over. Everyone left the classes.

SCOUT: Where did they go?

SCAMPER: They went into a big room. I jumped onto the windowsill so I could see.

SCOUT: *(giggles)* A squirrel looking into a church window is funny!

SCAMPER: *(giggles)* It was fun! They sang songs and prayed. Then the preacher read from the Bible and talked to the people.

SCOUT: He and the teachers are God's helpers. They tell us about Jesus.

SCAMPER: We can pray for people who tell about Jesus.

Discussion Questions

1. Who was teaching the children?
2. Where did Scamper sit to see the preacher?
3. What did the church people do while Peter was in prison?
4. How did God answer their prayers?
5. Who tells you about Jesus?
6. Who can you pray for because they tell about Jesus?

We Can Learn About Jesus

Based on: Acts 16—Lydia Follows Jesus
Props: none

SCOUT: *(sadly)* Hi, Scamper.

SCAMPER: Hi, Scout. You don't sound so happy today.

SCOUT: I'm not.

SCAMPER: Why?

SCOUT: The weatherman says it is going to rain!

SCAMPER: So?

SCOUT: If it rains, I can't play outside.

SCAMPER: Rain is not so bad, Scout.

SCOUT: It is if I can't be outside!

SCAMPER: You can play inside.

SCOUT: I planned to go to the pond!

SCAMPER: *(giggles)* Scout, you'll get wet at the pond anyway. Why worry about the rain?

SCOUT: My owners keep me indoors when it rains.

SCAMPER: Why?

SCOUT: They don't like muddy paw prints on the carpet.

SCAMPER: If you play at the pond, you'll have muddy paws.

SCOUT: Yeah, but I play on the grass afterwards. The grass wipes my feet clean.

SCAMPER: I see.

SCOUT: *(whining)* Why does it have to rain?

SCAMPER: The rain makes flowers and vegetables grow.

SCOUT: *(pouting)* But I want to play.

SCAMPER: Scout, *(emphasizes)* listen to me! If it never rained, everything would dry up. The trees wouldn't make nuts for me to eat.

SCOUT: Would the flowers die?

SCAMPER: All the flowers and all the gardens would die. There would be no grass.

SCOUT: No grass? Oh no! I need grass to wipe my muddy feet after I've been at the pond!

SCAMPER: We would miss the grass.

SCOUT: I like to lie in the cool grass on a hot day.

SCAMPER: Now you're learning about rain.

SCOUT: Let it rain! I'll play at the pond another day.

SCAMPER: *(pats Scout)* Good dog!

SCOUT: *(admiringly)* You are smart, Scamper. I'm glad I listened.

SCAMPER: *(looks at children)* The boys and girls are listening and learning too.

SCOUT: We all learn at church.

SCAMPER: We can learn about Jesus.

SCOUT: I'm all ears! *(flips ears by shaking head twice)*

Discussion Questions

1. What does Scout want to do?
2. What did Scout learn?
3. Where did Lydia meet Paul?
4. What did Lydia learn from the disciples?
5. When must you listen?
6. What have you learned from listening?

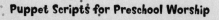

We Can Sing About Jesus

Based on: Acts 16—The Jailer Follows Jesus
Props: none

Scout: *(howling) Howl. Howl. Howl. (continues to howl through Scamper's next line)*

Scamper: *(tucks face down while reaching paws toward ears)* Scout, stop that!

Scout: *Howl. (stops howling)* What did you say?

Scamper: I said, stop making that noise!

Scout: *(surprised)* I wasn't making noise.

Scamper: Yes, you were. It sounded like *(imitates Scout) howl.*

Scout: Oh, that! I was singing.

Scamper: Singing?

Scout: Yes. I love to sing.

Scamper: So that's what I heard last night after dark!

Scout: I was singing, all right! I like to sing to the moon!

Scamper: *(giggles)* The moon probably heard you. It was a loud song.

Scout: I hope so.

Scamper: Dogs don't sing like the birds, do they?

Scout: Nope. We just sing like dogs.

Scamper: Could you please *(emphasizes) try* to sing like a bird?

Scout: I'll try. *(speaks in a high pitched, off-key voice) Tweet, tweet, tweet.*

Scamper: Hm. I guess you'd better stick to singing like a dog.

Scout: I guess that means you like to hear me sing. *Howl. Howl.*

Scamper: *(giggles)* I like it better than your bird song!

Scout: Good. *(giggles)* I don't think I'd like sitting on a branch. That's where the birds sing.

Scamper: You might fall off.

Scout: Scamper, can you sing?

Scamper: Not much. Squirrels mostly use their voices to chatter.

Scout: I heard you sing once. It was a song about Jesus.

Scamper: Oh yeah, sometimes I sing with the children.

Scout: I know some songs about Jesus.

Scamper: We can sing about Jesus.

Scout: Jesus songs are fun.

Scamper: Yep.

Scout: *(howls) Howl.*

Scamper: *(giggles)*

Discussion Questions

1. How does Scout sing?
2. What does Scout sing to at night?
3. What did Paul and Silas do while they were in the jail?
4. How did God set them free?
5. What happy songs do you like to sing?
6. Do you know any songs about Jesus?

We Can Help Others Learn About Jesus

Based on: Acts 28; Ephesians 4, 6; Philippians 1, 2; Colossians 4—Paul Helps People Follow Jesus

Props: Find an addressed envelope that is stamped and canceled. Names on the envelope won't matter.

SCAMPER:	Hi, Scout.
SCOUT:	*(holding envelope)* Hi! Our family got a letter!
SCAMPER:	Who from?
SCOUT:	The grandmother wrote it.
SCAMPER:	What was written in it?
SCOUT:	She wants to visit in the fall.
SCAMPER:	That will be nice. You like the grandmother, don't you?
SCOUT:	Very much! She rubs my ears.
SCAMPER:	It is fun to get letters from far away.
SCOUT:	She said something about me in the letter.
SCAMPER:	She did?
SCOUT:	She said she loved my soft fur.
SCAMPER:	*(feels Scout's fur)* You are soft, Scout.
SCOUT:	*(rubs stomach)* I am!
SCAMPER:	What else did the grandmother say?
SCOUT:	She will bring presents to everyone.
SCAMPER:	I guess that made the children happy!
SCOUT:	It sure did. It made me happy too.
SCAMPER:	*(surprised)* Are you getting a gift too?
SCOUT:	*(nodding)* She is bringing dog biscuits!
SCAMPER:	I know how you love those!
SCOUT:	I'll share with you, Scamper.
SCAMPER:	*(hesitates)* Uh, no thanks, Scout. I don't like dog food. You can have it all.
SCOUT:	*(giggles)* I forgot.
SCAMPER:	*(giggles)*
SCOUT:	The letter brought good news!
SCAMPER:	I'm glad you told me the good news.
SCOUT:	The Bible has good news too.
SCAMPER:	We learn about Jesus from the Bible.
SCOUT:	We can help others learn about Jesus too.
SCAMPER:	It is fun to tell good news!
SCOUT:	It is fun to write letters.
SCAMPER:	Go home, Scout. Write me a letter.
SCOUT:	I will. You write me back, OK?
SCAMPER:	OK, Scout. See you!

Discussion Questions

1. Who got a letter?
2. What did the grandmother promise to bring to Scout?
3. To whom did Paul send letters?
4. Who did Paul write about in his letters?
5. Have you gotten a letter or card in the mail?
6. To whom can you send a letter?

Jesus Loves Us All

Holiday: New Year's Day
Props: Place a calendar nearby.

SCAMPER: Happy New Year, Scout!

SCOUT: Same to you, Scamper.

SCAMPER: Isn't it exciting?

SCOUT: *(hesitantly)* Um . . . well . . . um . . . no.

SCAMPER: You're not excited to see the new year?

SCOUT: That's just it, Scamper. I can't *(emphasizes) see* it!

SCAMPER: *(giggles)* Of course you can't.

SCOUT: If you can't see it, how do you know it is here?

SCAMPER: We look at the calendar. Last year was *(year)*.

SCOUT: *(puzzled)* I still don't understand.

SCAMPER: There are lots of days on each calendar.

SCOUT: I know that.

SCAMPER: When we have used all the days on a calendar, we start a new year.

SCOUT: Then do you get a new calendar?

SCAMPER: Yep. We start all over again, counting the days.

SCOUT: A new calendar means a new year?

SCAMPER: You got it! This year is *(year)*. Today is the *(date)* day of the new year.

SCOUT: A year is a long time.

SCAMPER: Yes, but each year is special. We will have another Christmas.

SCOUT: How about Easter?

SCAMPER: Yep. We will each get another birthday too.

SCOUT: Wow! I love birthdays!

SCAMPER: Summer will come again.

SCOUT: People are happy to see a new year!

SCAMPER: Some people like to start over in other ways too.

SCOUT: How?

SCAMPER: They make mistakes sometimes. They want to try again to be good.

SCOUT: They don't want to give up.

SCAMPER: Jesus gives everyone another chance.

SCOUT: Jesus loves us all.

Discussion Questions

1. Who learned about calendars?
2. When do we start over with a new year?
3. What do we call the holiday when we start a new calendar?
4. What year is this?
5. Can you name a holiday we will celebrate again this year?
6. How old will you be on your birthday this year?

God Showed His Love for People

Holiday: Valentine's Day

Props: Make two construction paper Valentines. On one, write "I'm nuts over you. Love, Scamper." Draw or glue a picture of an acorn on the front. On the other, write, "My Tail Wags for You! Love, Scout." Draw or glue a picture of a dog on the front. (See the clip art on pages 135 and 136 for possible images of Scout to use on this card.) Glue the end of a small cardboard strip to the back of each card. Bend the cardboard strips to make stands for the cards so that they stand upright. Place them within the children's view.

SCAMPER: (looks at valentine from Scout) Thank you for the great valentine, Scout!

SCOUT: You're welcome. Do you understand it?

SCAMPER: Let me read it again. (looks at valentine) "My tail wags for you!"

SCOUT: I'm always happy to see you. Get it?

SCAMPER: I get it, Scout. You show your friendship by wagging your tail!

SCOUT: You are my (emphasizes) best pal, Scamper.

SCAMPER: (hugs Scout) I know.

SCOUT: (looks at valentine from Scamper) Thank you for making a valentine for me.

SCAMPER: (excited) I (emphasizes) knew you would like an acorn on yours!

SCOUT: I do. Acorns remind me of you. You like nuts.

SCAMPER: Yep. Do you get it? (reads valentine) "Nuts over you?"

SCOUT: (giggles) I got it. It means you are crazy about me.

SCAMPER: It means I like you. We are buddies.

SCOUT: Valentine's Day is fun.

SCAMPER: People send valentines too.

SCOUT: My owner bought candy for his wife and children.

SCAMPER: Yummy.

SCOUT: The florist brought flowers to a neighbor.

SCAMPER: Wow. People really like to celebrate, don't they?

SCOUT: They give things to show their love.

SCAMPER: God showed His love for people.

SCOUT: He did. (thoughtfully) He gave Jesus to the world.

SCAMPER: (softly) Jesus was the (emphasizes) best gift of all!

SCOUT: Happy Valentine's Day, Scamper!

SCAMPER: Happy Valentine's Day to you, Scout! (Scout and Scamper hug)

Discussion Questions

1. What special day are Scout and Scamper celebrating?
2. What did Scout make for Scamper?
3. What does "I'm nuts over you" mean?
4. Who do you love?
5. How will you celebrate Valentine's Day?
6. For whom can you make a valentine?

God Planned for Families

Holiday: Mother's Day
Props: none

SCAMPER: Oh-oh. It must be a special day.

SCOUT: Why do you think so?

SCAMPER: I see many ladies wearing flowers.

SCOUT: You're right, Scamper. It is a holiday.

SCAMPER: What holiday is it?

SCOUT: Mother's Day.

SCAMPER: Why is there a Mother's Day?

SCOUT: It is so people can show love to mothers.

SCAMPER: Mothers are very special.

SCOUT: Yes, they are. That's why there is a Mother's Day.

SCAMPER: Mothers know everything!

SCOUT: They seem to.

SCAMPER: My mom knows when I have been bad.

SCOUT: *(giggles)* Mothers know a lot.

SCAMPER: They must be perfect.

SCOUT: Nah. Nobody's perfect.

SCAMPER: Not even mothers?

SCOUT: Not even mothers. They are just like everyone else.

SCAMPER: Then why do we have the holiday?

SCOUT: Because mothers do things for their families.

SCAMPER: They do a lot for us.

SCOUT: The mother at my house is always working.

SCAMPER: What does she do?

SCOUT: She cooks food for the family.

SCAMPER: Is it delicious?

SCOUT: Usually, but sometimes the girl complains.

SCAMPER: Does the mother get mad when the girl gripes?

SCOUT: No, she just says, "You'll eat when you are hungry."

SCAMPER: Does the girl eat the food?

SCOUT: She always does, so it can't be too bad.

SCAMPER: What else does the mother do?

SCOUT: She cleans house. She makes the children pick up toys.

SCAMPER: She makes them *(emphasizes) work?*

SCOUT: Of course, it is their mess. They should clean it up.

SCAMPER: The mother could do it.

SCOUT: She won't do that. She teaches the children to obey family rules.

SCAMPER: Even the baby?

SCOUT: He can pick up one or two toys. He is learning.

SCAMPER: Families can work together.

SCOUT: The Bible tells about God's plan for families.

SCAMPER: Mothers are God's helpers.

SCOUT: That's why there is a Mother's Day!

Discussion Questions

1. Who is wearing flowers?
2. Who planned for families?
3. What book tells about God's plan for families?
4. What does your mother do for you?
5. How can you help your mother?
6. What special thing can you do for your grandmother or another family member?

Families Love One Another

Holiday: Father's Day
Props: none

SCAMPER: Today is a holiday.

SCOUT: Yep, it's Father's Day.

SCAMPER: How do you know?

SCOUT: I found out this morning. The children woke up their father.

SCAMPER: I guess he didn't like that!

SCOUT: Yes, he did. They were telling him, "Happy Father's Day!"

SCAMPER: Why?

SCOUT: Today is Father's Day. It is a good day to show love to fathers.

SCAMPER: What did the children do?

SCOUT: They gave him a present.

SCAMPER: What did he get?

SCOUT: First the girl gave him a card she made at school.

SCAMPER: Did the baby boy give him a gift?

SCOUT: His mother gave him a pencil to scribble on the card.

SCAMPER: *(giggles)* He's too little write his own name.

SCOUT: The father liked it anyway.

SCAMPER: The cards were a nice surprise for the father.

SCOUT: He opened his present too.

SCAMPER: What did he get?

SCOUT: Some tools.

SCAMPER: I wouldn't like tools! I would want toys!

SCOUT: You are not a father. Fathers like tools.

SCAMPER: They do? How strange.

SCOUT: *(giggles)* Believe me, Scamper. He was very happy with tools!

SCAMPER: Good. I noticed the men in church smiling today.

SCOUT: Many of them are fathers.

SCAMPER: I wonder if they all got gifts?

SCOUT: I saw a *(emphasizes) lot* of new neckties!

SCAMPER: Who would want a necktie?

SCOUT: It's not so much about what they *(emphasizes) want*. They are happy because it is a gift from their children.

SCAMPER: They must love their kids a lot!

SCOUT: They do. God wants families to love one another.

SCAMPER: The Bible says to love one another.

SCOUT: *(looks at children)* Children can show love to their families.

SCAMPER: I love my dad. I think I'll give him some corn.

SCOUT: *(giggles)* He'd trip on a necktie, anyway!

SCAMPER: *(giggles)*

Discussion Questions

1. What holiday is today?
2. What does God want you to feel for your family?
3. What important book tells us to love each other?
4. How does your family celebrate holidays?
5. How can you thank God for your family?
6. What special thing can you do for your father or grandfather?

We Can Thank God for Our Country

Holiday: Patriotic
Props: Place a small flag standing nearby.

SCAMPER: Are you ready for the parade?

SCOUT: Yep. It is going to pass right by my yard!

SCAMPER: Really? That's exciting!

SCOUT: You can come, Scamper. You can sit by me.

SCAMPER: OK, Scout. Are you sure you will sit still and watch?

SCOUT: *(hesitantly)* Um . . . I will. *(pauses)* That is, I will as long as I can.

SCAMPER: You will until you get too excited.

SCOUT: *(giggles)* Then I will jump and bark!

SCAMPER: *(giggles)* Dogs love to bark.

SCOUT: *(happily)* I do. I will wag my tail while the music plays.

SCAMPER: You're not going to sing, are you?

SCOUT: No. My owner would tell me to sit and be quiet.

SCAMPER: *(giggles)* I'm sure he would!

SCOUT: Do you know why there is a parade today?

SCAMPER: I thought it was just for fun.

SCOUT: It is fun, but there is a reason.

SCAMPER: What reason?

SCOUT: This parade is to honor our country!

SCAMPER: I'm glad to live in this country.

SCOUT: So am I, Scamper. I like living here.

SCAMPER: We can thank God for our country.

(both puppets salute flag)

Discussion Questions

1. Why is there a parade?
2. Where will Scamper sit to watch the parade?
3. What will Scout do when he gets excited?
4. Have you seen a parade?
5. What do you like about your country?
6. How can you thank God for your country?

Jesus Is the Light of the World

Holiday: Halloween

Props: Place a small lit pumpkin nearby. The light may be electric, battery, or candle powered.

SCOUT: *(looks at pumpkin)* Look, Scamper! A pumpkin with a face!

SCAMPER: *(looks at pumpkin)* It's a happy face too! Cool!

SCOUT: Yes, and it is shining!

SCAMPER: *(looks closely at pumpkin)* What makes it so bright?

SCOUT: I'll find out. *(looks inside pumpkin)* I can see inside the pumpkin.

SCAMPER: What's in there?

SCOUT: *(still examining pumpkin)* There is a light inside.

SCAMPER: Let me see. *(looks inside pumpkin)* I see it! It is a very bright light.

SCOUT: It's like a flashlight inside a little room.

SCAMPER: Some of the light is spilling out of its face.

SCOUT: *(looks at pumpkin)* You're right, Scamper! I see light shining through its eyes!

SCAMPER: *(stands back and looks at pumpkin)* Light is coming from its mouth too.

SCOUT: I like this pumpkin.

SCAMPER: I do too. Its light makes the pumpkin's smile shine brightly.

SCOUT: I know another kind of light.

SCAMPER: You do? What is it?

SCOUT: Jesus. The Bible says Jesus is the light of the world.

SCAMPER: Why do you think it says that?

SCOUT: Well, Jesus told people about God.

SCAMPER: Jesus is full of love. I think people saw love shining in His eyes.

SCOUT: He spoke of love with His smiling mouth.

SCAMPER: So Jesus lights the world with love! *(claps paws)* Hooray for Jesus!

SCOUT: *(looks at children)* The children can light the world with Jesus' love too.

SCAMPER: How?

SCOUT: They can be kind to someone who is hurt.

SCAMPER: Children can tell others about Jesus.

SCOUT: They can say "I love you" to someone.

SCAMPER: It's nice to be loved.

SCOUT: It makes us feel happy.

SCAMPER: Just like the pumpkin's face!

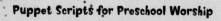

Discussion Questions

1. Where was the light shining out of the pumpkin?
2. Where do we read about Jesus' love?
3. How does Jesus light the world?
4. What can you say to make someone happy?
5. How can you show Jesus' love to others?
6. How do you feel when someone shows you love?

We Can Thank God In Many Ways

Holiday: Thanksgiving
Props: none

SCAMPER: Hi, Scout.

SCOUT: Hi.

SCAMPER: I fell out of my tree yesterday.

SCOUT: You did? Were you hurt?

SCAMPER: I only was bruised.

SCOUT: *(touches Scamper's paw)* Did you bleed?

SCAMPER: Nope.

SCOUT: Not even a little bit?

SCAMPER: Nope.

SCOUT: Did you get a bandage?

SCAMPER: No, I didn't need one.

SCOUT: You are a lucky squirrel!

SCAMPER: I know. I could have been hurt.

SCOUT: The Bible says God sees the sparrow when it falls.

SCAMPER: I wonder if He saw me.

SCOUT: He loves all His animals. He sees them all.

SCAMPER: God loves people and animals.

SCOUT: God made a beautiful world.

SCAMPER: We can thank Him for the world.

SCOUT: I'm thankful for my home and people who love me.

SCAMPER: We can thank God for our homes.

SCOUT: And for people who love us too.

SCAMPER: What else are you thankful for, Scout?

SCOUT: Food! I love my Puppy Crunch!

SCAMPER: I like to eat corn and nuts!

SCOUT: We can thank God for food.

SCAMPER: How do people thank God?

SCOUT: They pray.

SCAMPER: The children pray at church.

SCOUT: At my house, the girl prays before going to bed.

SCAMPER: Does she start by saying, "Now I lay me down to sleep"?

SCOUT: How did you know?

SCAMPER: Lots of children say that prayer.

SCOUT: How else can children thank God?

SCAMPER: They can show thankfulness by obeying.

SCOUT: How about by helping others?

SCAMPER: That is another good way.

SCOUT: I can thank God with a song. *(howls)* Howl. Howl.

SCAMPER: *(giggles)* You sure can, Scout!

SCOUT: We can thank God in many ways.

Discussion Questions

1. Why didn't Scamper need a bandage?
2. How does Scout sing?
3. Who sees a sparrow if it falls?
4. Can you say a bedtime prayer?
5. What are you most thankful for?
6. How can you thank God?

We Can Give Thanks to God

Holiday: Thanksgiving
Props: none

SCOUT: Hi, Scamper!

SCAMPER: Hi, Scout. What can we play today?

SCOUT: Let's play the alphabet game.

SCAMPER: OK. Let's say what we are thankful for this time.

SCOUT: You go first.

SCAMPER: *A.* I am thankful for acorns! I love nuts!

SCOUT: *B. B* is for ball, my favorite toy.

SCAMPER: *C. C* is for crayons. I like to color with crayons.

SCOUT: *D* is for dog! I'm a dog!

SCAMPER: I'm thankful for you, Scout.

SCOUT: Your turn!

SCAMPER: *E. E* is for earth. This is a great world.

SCOUT: OK. *F* is next. I'm thankful for *(pauses)* fish! I like fish.

SCAMPER: Let me see, *G.* I know. Game! I like this game.

SCOUT: *H* is for holiday! I'm thankful for holidays.

SCAMPER: It is getting harder. What begins with *I*? Um . . . ice.

SCOUT: I like ice. I eat it. You go again, Scamper.

SCAMPER: OK. *J* is for jump! I'm thankful I can jump.

SCOUT: You jump far, Scamper.

SCAMPER: *(giggles)* It is fun to jump from tree to tree!

SCOUT: My turn. *K* is for kiss. *(kisses Scamper)* Smack!

SCAMPER: *(giggles)* I like kisses too. *L* is for log.

SCOUT: Why are you thankful for a log?

SCAMPER: I use a log for a picnic table. That's where I sit to eat nuts.

SCOUT: Oh. *(pauses)* I'm thankful for the minister! Minister starts with *M*.

SCAMPER: We can thank him. He loves the church.

SCOUT: *N* is for neighbor. You are my neighbor. I am thankful for you.

SCAMPER: Thank you, Scout. I'm getting tired. Let's stop playing for now.

SCOUT: OK. We are really thankful, aren't we?

SCAMPER: We are thankful for lots of things!

SCOUT: We can give thanks to God.

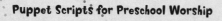

Discussion Questions

1. What game did Scout and Scamper play?
2. What is the first letter in the alphabet?
3. Can you say the alphabet?
4. Name one thing for which you can thank God.
5. Name one person you are thankful for?
6. How can you thank someone?

God Made Our World

Holiday: Fall
Props: none

SCAMPER: Hi, Scout.

SCOUT: Hi, Scamper. Have you seen the trees?

SCAMPER: Do you mean the new colors?

SCOUT: Yeah. They used to be green!

SCAMPER: Now they are red, yellow, and orange!

SCOUT: I can see that. Why did they change colors?

SCAMPER: It is fall now. It is time for everything to change.

SCOUT: Why?

SCAMPER: The leaves have dressed in their prettiest colors for a big party.

SCOUT: Leaves have parties?

SCAMPER: They are partying now. See them dancing in the wind?

SCOUT: *(looks out window)* Hey, they *(emphasizes) are* dancing!

SCAMPER: They will wear those bright colors all season.

SCOUT: That sounds like fun. What are they celebrating?

SCAMPER: Harvest time.

SCOUT: *(whining)* Scamper, puppies have so much to learn! What is a harvest?

SCAMPER: That's when all the vegetables are ripe.

SCOUT: I saw lots of pumpkins in a yard. Were they picked for the harvest?

SCAMPER: Yep! Pumpkins and corn are a part of the harvest.

SCOUT: That makes you happy, because you like corn.

SCAMPER: Yummy! *(rubs stomach)* I get lots of corn to eat.

SCOUT: The trees look happy.

SCAMPER: Everyone is happy.

SCOUT: When the party is over, will the trees wear green again?

SCAMPER: Nope. The colored leaves will fall to the ground.

SCOUT: Why?

SCAMPER: They are getting ready for their winter rest. Then it all starts over again!

SCOUT: With green leaves?

SCAMPER: That's right. It always happens that way. You can count on it.

SCOUT: How do you know?

SCAMPER: My mom told me that God planned it that way.

SCOUT: Wow! God had some cool ideas!

SCAMPER: God made our world.

SCOUT: I like all the colors!

SCAMPER: This is a beautiful time of year!

SCOUT: Look outside. There are some colored leaves all piled up!

SCAMPER: Come on, Scout. I'll show you how to have fun in leaves!

Discussion Questions

1. What harvest vegetable does Scamper like?
2. What do you think Scout and Scamper are going to do in the leaves?
3. Who planned the fall season?
4. In your yard are the leaves changing colors?
5. What is your favorite leaf color?
6. How do you play with leaves?

We Can Praise God for Good Things

Holiday: Winter
Props: none

SCOUT: Did you see the snow falling from the sky?

SCAMPER: I sure did! I like to *(bounces)* jump in it!

SCOUT: So do I!

SCAMPER: I saw a snowman in your yard.

SCOUT: The girl and her dad made it.

SCAMPER: It is big!

SCOUT: It has a hat and scarf.

SCAMPER: *(giggles)* Snowmen are supposed to be cold! They don't need scarves and hats.

SCOUT: *(giggles)*

SCAMPER: Did you help build the snowman?

SCOUT: Nope. I ran in circles, wagged my tail, and dug in the snow. It was fun!

SCAMPER: I wonder if the snowman will come alive.

SCOUT: Why would you think that?

SCAMPER: You've heard the song, "Frosty the Snowman"!

SCOUT: Silly Scamper. Snowmen can't come alive.

SCAMPER: Frosty did.

SCOUT: Not for real. It is just a fun song.

SCAMPER: *(disappointed)* Oh.

SCOUT: Don't feel bad, Scamper. *(pats Scamper)*

SCAMPER: It is a good song, even if it is just for fun.

SCOUT: Yep.

SCAMPER: Sing it for me, Scout.

SCOUT: *(howls)* Howl. Howl.

SCAMPER: *(reaching for ears and tucking head down)* Never mind! You don't have to sing.

SCOUT: *(giggles)* I like to sing.

SCAMPER: *(giggles)*

SCOUT: Winter is fun. We can play in the snow.

SCAMPER: We can slide down the hill!

SCOUT: I like to hide in the snow.

SCAMPER: I dig in the snow.

SCOUT: Why do you do that?

SCAMPER: My nuts are hidden in the ground. I dig them up in the winter.

SCOUT: I forgot about that.

SCAMPER: God made the snow.

SCOUT: God made the whole world! We can read about it in the Bible.

Discussion Questions

1. What does Scout do in the snow?
2. What song did Scamper know about a snowman?
3. Where can we read about God making the world?
4. In the winter what do you put on to go outdoors?
5. Do we have snow where we live?
6. How can you praise God for winter?

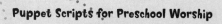

God Planned Springtime

Holiday: Spring
Props: Place a toy frog nearby.

SCAMPER: Hey, Scout! See the frog?

SCOUT: *(looks at toy)* Yeah. It's a cute frog, Scamper.

SCAMPER: I saw a real frog this morning!

SCOUT: You did? Where?

SCAMPER: It was clinging to my tree.

SCOUT: Did it say hello?

SCAMPER: *(giggles)* Frogs can't talk. It said *(imitates frog)* Croak!

SCOUT: *(giggles)* You are a funny sounding frog!

SCAMPER: I'm glad the frogs are back. They were gone all winter.

SCOUT: They have been asleep.

SCAMPER: Where do frogs sleep?

SCOUT: In the mud.

SCAMPER: Yuk! Mud is dirty.

SCOUT: They sleep all winter in their soft mud home.

SCAMPER: *(giggles)* I guess they need a bath before breakfast!

SCOUT: *(giggles)* I think they get clean in the water.

SCAMPER: Why do they sleep so long?

SCOUT: The winter is too cold for them.

SCAMPER: They could move to Florida where it is warm.

SCOUT: It is too far for most of them to walk.

SCAMPER: They could fly.

SCOUT: Frogs aren't allowed on airplanes.

SCAMPER: I guess they *(emphasizes) have* to stay here. They *(emphasizes) have* to find a warm place to sleep.

SCOUT: Lots of animals sleep all winter.

SCAMPER: Which ones?

SCOUT: Bears sleep. So do snakes and turtles.

SCAMPER: When do they wake up?

SCOUT: In the springtime.

SCAMPER: How do they wake up? Does an alarm ring when it is spring?

SCOUT: No. *(giggles)* Silly Scamper.

SCAMPER: How do they know it is time to get up?

SCOUT: The sun shines warmly.

SCAMPER: When sun shines into my tree, I know it is morning.

SCOUT: The animals feel the warm air and know it is spring.

SCAMPER: How about the flowers?

SCOUT: The sun makes them warm too.

SCAMPER: It melts the snow and ice.

SCOUT: *(emphasizes) Everything* wakes up in the spring.

SCAMPER: Animals and flowers.

SCOUT: Trees grow leaves and grass turns green.

SCAMPER: God planned springtime.

SCOUT: He made a beautiful world!

Discussion Questions

1. What did the frog say?
2. Who wakes the sleeping animals and flowers?
3. Who made the world?
4. What wakes you?
5. What do you like best about spring?
6. Do you have any flowers in your yard that wake up in the spring?

We Can Thank God for the World

Holiday: Summer
Props: none

SCAMPER: Hi, Scout.

SCOUT: Hi, Scamper.

SCAMPER: It sure is a hot day.

SCOUT: Yep. Someone said that these are the dog days of summer.

SCAMPER: What does that mean?

SCOUT: I don't know.

SCAMPER: You are a *(emphasizes)* dog! You should know.

SCOUT: I think it means that dogs like summertime.

SCAMPER: Do you like summer?

SCOUT: It is my favorite time of year!

SCAMPER: Because it is warm and you can play outside?

SCOUT: Yep. Summer is nice.

SCAMPER: What do you play in the summertime?

SCOUT: I play hide-and-seek with you.

SCAMPER: That is fun.

SCOUT: We play tag.

SCAMPER: We both run fast when we play tag.

SCOUT: I like to go to the pond.

SCAMPER: What do you do there?

SCOUT: I watch the fish.

SCAMPER: And frogs?

SCOUT: Frogs too. I like to splash in the water!

SCAMPER: I know. You shake water off your fur, and I get wet!

SCOUT: *(giggles)* It is funny, Scamper.

SCAMPER: *(giggles)* I don't mind getting wet.

SCOUT: Why do you like summer, Scamper?

SCAMPER: I like summer because the whole world looks pretty.

SCOUT: The sky is a nice blue.

SCAMPER: Sometimes there are fluffy white clouds.

SCOUT: They look soft. I like flowers too.

SCAMPER: Flowers have lots of colors.

SCOUT: I like red best of all!

SCAMPER: Yellow. Yellow is my favorite.

SCOUT: What flower is yellow?

SCAMPER: Dandelions.

SCOUT: Oh yeah.

SCAMPER: God made the flowers.

SCOUT: We can praise God for the world.

SCAMPER: OK, Scout, lets go play.

SCOUT: It is the fun dog days of summer!

Discussion Questions

1. What is Scout's favorite time of year?
2. Why does Scamper like summer?
3. Who made the flowers?
4. What kind of weather do we have in summer?
5. What outdoor games do you like to play?
6. What do you like about summer that you can praise God for?

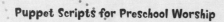

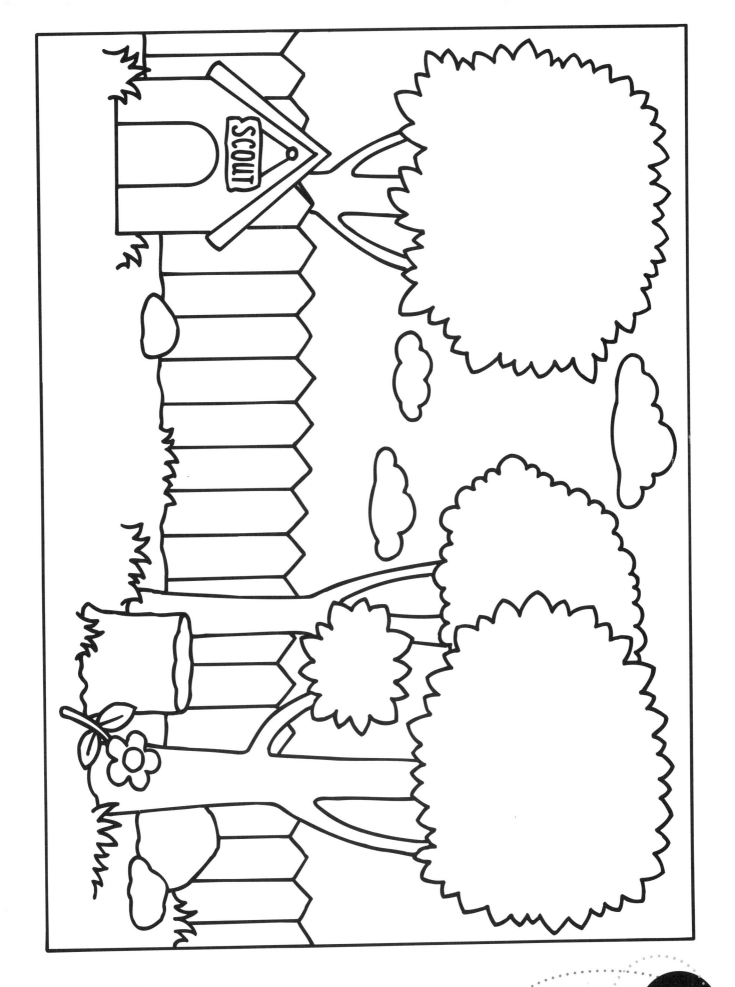

The sign on the doghouse reads: SCOUT

Puppet Scripts for Preschool Worship

Scamper Clip Art

Use these images of Scamper to

- make stick puppets of Scamper for the children so that they can follow along with the script or make up their own,
- project images of Scamper onto the wall during the scripts using an overhead projector and the clip art copied onto transparencies, or
- create fun announcements or take-home papers with images of Scamper right on each page.

Puppet Scripts for Preschool Worship

Scout Clip Art

Use these images of Scout to

- make stick puppets of Scout for the children so that they can follow along with the script or make up their own,
- project images of Scout onto the wall during the scripts using an overhead projector and the clip art copied onto transparencies, or
- create fun announcements or take-home papers with images of Scout right on each page.

Puppet Scripts for Preschool Worship

Topical Index

Learn and Grow

Obey/Follow

Please God

Pray

Tell About God/Jesus

Thanks and Praise

The Bible

Trust God/Jesus

Worship

HeartShaper™ Preschool/Pre-K & K Scope & Sequence

Fall Year 1
God Made the Sky and Earth (p. 15)
God Made Fish and Birds (p. 16)
God Made Animals (p. 17)
God Made People (p. 19)
Noah Builds a Boat (p. 23)
Noah and the Flood (p. 24)
Abram Moves (p. 25)
Abram and Lot (p. 26)
Abraham and Sarah Have a Baby (p. 27)
Joseph as a Boy (p. 28)
Joseph Serves God All His Life (p. 29)
Samuel as a Boy (p. 41)
Samuel Serves God All His Life (p. 42)

Winter Year 1
An Angel Announces Jesus' Birth (p. 67)
Jesus Is Born (p. 69)
Shepherds Visit Jesus (p. 72)
Simeon and Anna See Jesus (p. 73)
Wise Men Worship Jesus (p. 75)
Jesus as a Boy (p. 76)
Jesus Is Baptized (p. 77)
Jesus Is Tempted (p. 78)
Jesus Begins to Teach (p. 82)
Jesus and the Children (p. 102)
Jesus and Matthew (p. 85)
Jesus and a Woman from Samaria (p. 80)
Jesus and Zacchaeus (p. 104)

Spring Year 1
Triumphal Entry: People Praise Jesus (p. 106)
Resurrection Sunday: Jesus Lives! (p. 108)
Jesus Heals an Official's Son (p. 81)
Jesus Heals a Man Who Could Not Walk (p. 84)
Jesus Heals the Soldier's Servant (p. 88)
Jesus Brings a Young Man Back to Life (p. 89)
Jesus Walks on Water (p. 93)
Jesus Heals a Man Who Could Not Hear or Speak (p. 94)
The Church Begins (p. 109)
Peter and John at the Temple (p. 111)
Phillip Tells About Jesus (p. 112)
Peter and Tabitha (p. 114)
The Church Prays for Peter in Prison (115)

Summer Year 1
David Plays for Saul (p. 43)
David Meets Goliath (p. 44)
David and Jonathan (p. 45)
David and Mephibosheth (p. 46)
David Sings to God (p. 47)
Solomon Prays to Know What Is Right (p. 48)
Solomon Builds the Temple (p. 49)
Jehoshaphat Asks for God's Help (p. 59)
Josiah Reads God's Word (p. 58)
Elisha and a Widow's Oil (p. 54)
Elisha and a Shunammite Family (p. 55)
Elisha and the Shunammite's Son (p. 56)
Elisha and Naaman (p. 57)

HeartShaper™ Preschool/Pre-K & K Scope & Sequence

Fall Year 2
God Made a World for People (p. 18)
God Made Adam and Eve (p. 20)
God Made My Senses (p. 21)
God Made Me Special (p. 22)
Moses Is Born (p. 30)
Moses Leads God's People (p. 31)
God's People Cross the Red Sea (p. 32)
God Provides for His People (p. 33)
God Gives Ten Rules (p. 34)
Joshua and Caleb (p. 35)
God's People Cross the Jordan River (p. 36)
The Fall of Jericho (p. 37)
Joshua Talks to God's People (p. 38)

Winter Year 2
An Angel Brings Special News (p. 68)
A Special Baby Is Born (p. 70)
Shepherds Hear Special News (p. 71)
Wise Men Worship a Special Baby (p. 74)
Jesus Teaches About Pleasing God (p. 86)
Jesus Teaches About Giving (p. 87)
Jesus Teaches About Praying (p. 98)
Jesus Teaches About Helping (p. 96)
Jesus Teaches About Sharing (p. 99)
Two Friends Follow Jesus (p. 79)
Fishermen Follow Jesus (p. 83)
Mary and Martha Follow Jesus (p. 97)
Bartimaeus Follows Jesus (p. 103)

Spring Year 2
Triumphal Entry: A Crowd Welcomes Jesus (p. 105)
Resurrection Sunday: Jesus Is Alive (p. 107)
Jesus Stops a Storm (p. 90)
Jesus Heals a Young Girl (p. 91)
Jesus Feeds a Crowd (p. 92)
Jesus Heals a Man Born Blind (p. 95)
Jesus Heals 10 Men (p. 101)
Jesus Brings Lazarus Back to Life (p. 100)
The Church Follows Jesus (p. 110)
Saul Begins to Follow Jesus (p. 113)
Lydia Follows Jesus (p. 116)
The Jailer Follows Jesus (p. 117)
Paul Helps People Follow Jesus (p. 118)

Summer Year 2
Elijah Is Fed by Ravens (p. 50)
Elijah Helps a Widow (p. 51)
Elijah Helps a Widow's Son (p. 52)
Elijah and the Prophets of Baal (p. 53)
Daniel and His Friends Obey God (p. 62)
Daniel's Friends Worship Only God (p. 63)
Daniel and the Handwriting on the Wall (p. 64)
Daniel and the Lions' Den (p. 65)
Gideon Lead's God's Army (p. 39)
Ruth Makes Good Choices (p. 40)
Jonah Tells About God (p. 66)
Esther Helps God's People (p. 61)
Nehemiah Rebuilds the Wall (p. 60)